Reduce. Reuse.
RECYCLE.

CW01500053

A decade ago, Atlantic Publishing signed the Green Press Initiative. These guidelines promote environmentally friendly practices, such as using recycled stock and vegetable-based inks, avoiding waste, choosing energy-efficient resources, and promoting a no-pulping policy. We now use 100-percent recycled stock on all our books. The results: in one year, switching to post-consumer recycled stock saved 24 mature trees, 5,000 gallons of water, the equivalent of the total energy used for one home in a year, and the equivalent of the greenhouse gases from one car driven for a year.

Over the years, we have adopted a number of dogs from rescues and shelters. First there was Bear and after he passed, Ginger and Scout. Now, we have Kira, another rescue. They have brought immense joy and love not just into our lives, but into the lives of all who met them.

We want you to know a portion of the profits of this book will be donated in Bear, Ginger and Scout's memory to local animal shelters, parks, conservation organizations, and other individuals and nonprofit organizations in need of assistance.

– Douglas & Sherri Brown,
President & Vice-President of Atlantic Publishing

This book is dedicated to Suzan who for 40 years put up with so much, but through it all remained calm and focused. She remains my very best friend, and I wish to sincerely apologize to her for all I put her through.

To Donald —
Thank you for being the
most wonderful friend —
52 years and counting!

SUNSET: SUNRISE

A Journey of Self-Acceptance

Enjoy the read —

By Sarah L. Hartley

With much love,
Sarah xx
April 2019

SUNSET: SUNRISE

Copyright © 2017 Atlantic Publishing Group, Inc.

1405 SW 6th Avenue • Ocala, Florida 34471 • Phone 800-814-1132 • Fax 352-622-1875
Website: www.atlantic-pub.com • Email: sales@atlantic-pub.com
SAN Number: 268-1250

No part of this publication may be reproduced, stored in a retrieval system, or transmitted in any form or by any means, electronic, mechanical, photocopying, recording, scanning, or otherwise, except as permitted under Section 107 or 108 of the 1976 United States Copyright Act, without the prior written permission of the Publisher. Requests to the Publisher for permission should be sent to Atlantic Publishing Group, Inc., 1405 SW 6th Avenue, Ocala, Florida 34471.

Library of Congress Cataloging-in-Publication Data

Names: Hartley, Sarah L., author.
Title: Sunset: sunrise : an extraordinary odyssey / by Sarah L. Hartley.
Description: Ocala, Florida : Atlantic Publishing Group, Inc, [2017]
Identifiers: LCCN 2017046772 (print) | LCCN 2017053626 (ebook) | ISBN 9781620235058 (ebook) | ISBN 9781620235041 (paperback : alk. paper) | ISBN 1620235048 (alk. paper)
Subjects: LCSH: Hartley, Sarah L. | Transgender people—Biography—Anecdotes. | Manic-depressive illness—Patients—Biography—Anecdotes. | Transsexualism.
Classification: LCC HQ77.8.H373 (ebook) | LCC HQ77.8.H373 A3 2017 (print) | DDC 306.76/8—dc23
LC record available at https://lccn.loc.gov/2017046772

LIMIT OF LIABILITY/DISCLAIMER OF WARRANTY: The publisher and the author make no representations or warranties with respect to the accuracy or completeness of the contents of this work and specifically disclaim all warranties, including without limitation warranties of fitness for a particular purpose. No warranty may be created or extended by sales or promotional materials. The advice and strategies contained herein may not be suitable for every situation. This work is sold with the understanding that the publisher is not engaged in rendering legal, accounting, or other professional services. If professional assistance is required, the services of a competent professional should be sought. Neither the publisher nor the author shall be liable for damages arising herefrom. The fact that an organization or Web site is referred to in this work as a citation and/or a potential source of further information does not mean that the author or the publisher endorses the information the organization or Web site may provide or recommendations it may make. Further, readers should be aware that Internet Web sites listed in this work may have changed or disappeared between when this work was written and when it is read.

TRADEMARK DISCLAIMER: All trademarks, trade names, or logos mentioned or used are the property of their respective owners and are used only to directly describe the products being provided. Every effort has been made to properly capitalize, punctuate, identify, and attribute trademarks and trade names to their respective owners, including the use of ® and ™ wherever possible and practical. Atlantic Publishing Group, Inc. is not a partner, affiliate, or licensee with the holders of said trademarks.

Printed in the United States

PROJECT MANAGER: Danielle Lieneman
INTERIOR LAYOUT, COVER, AND JACKET DESIGN: Nicole Sturk

PERSEVERANTIA VINCIT

PERSEVERANCE CONQUERS

We all like good anecdotes, especially if they are true. Because my father died when I was aged 13, I always felt that I missed out on many of his stories and lessons learned. It is time to put to writing some of the stories and lessons I have learned along the way. Somehow a few short stories intended for my children, Deb and Jeremy, turned into a book about some of the darkest parts of my life that ultimately led to a true transformation. What originally was going to take a few months has turned into a few years.

Here we are: one person's life, no one of fame or fortune, but just one person with many life experiences.

ACKNOWLEDGMENTS

When I started thinking about the acknowledgements I should make I could come up with only a few names. Obviously, Suzan who played a major role in my life and still does; my late mother, Dorrie, and other members of my family who gave me much needed encouragement along the way. Also, David Howell who persuaded me to finish the book that remained partially written for the longest time and Danielle Lieneman, my editor, who has skillfully guided me into making the book comprehensible. My sincere thanks and gratitude go to all of them.

But when I started think more about it, I realized that I should say a huge thank you to all the people mention in the book, likable or not, for without them I would have had little to write about.

As my life unfolded in various countries, so did my use of the English language. For those readers trying to pick out spelling errors please remember that I have adjusted the spelling of words to match the countries in which I was located!

It should be mentioned that Wikipedia provided me with all sorts of factual and historical data. Some of the names of persons mentioned in this book have been changed to protect their identity.

I hope that you enjoy reading the book as much as I have enjoyed writing it.

TABLE OF CONTENTS

PART 1
CHILDHOOD

CHAPTER 1

CHILDHOOD MEMORIES

Chaddesley Corbett is a picturesque village in the County of Worcestershire in England. The main street is made up of old cottages built with black wooden beams and white plaster. Nowadays, all the cottages are beautifully maintained with well-kept gardens, but it wasn't always so. In the 1950s, Mrs. Rudd and her daughter, Rose, my mother's charwomen, lived in the village. They lived in a small cottage with an outside privy at the back. Cooking was carried out on a cast iron, coal-fired cooker, and they boiled water over the open fire by hanging pots on the metal supports. Although this might sound archaic, the cottage always seemed warm and welcoming, as was Mrs. Rudd. When she died, having never moved more than five miles away from Chaddesley in her 80-plus years, her cottage and the two next door were turned into very nice houses by adding onto the back while maintaining the oak beam structure on the interior and beautiful facade. Over the years, a working class village turned into an upper middle class one.

The villagers were well served by two village stores, a baker, a butcher, a barber, post office, cobbler, a parochial school, and three pubs. A typical English church with a spire and a beautiful lych gate adorns one end of the village. The villagers were lucky enough to have their own vicar and doctor. I have many memories of Jukes', the most popular village store. I was in awe with how the bulk goods such as flour or sugar were carefully weighed out, put into brown bags, and folded in a neat, tight way to prevent any spillage. I remember the long strip of sticky brown paper hanging down the middle of the store to catch the flies. One could always see a fly stuck to the paper, slowly dying as it struggled to get away. Besides being a convenience store for the villagers, it was also a place where one would often bump into friends and acquaintances and catch up on the local gossip. Village life was quiet and laid back, so it was all the more shocking when the villagers learned that Mr. Jukes, the baker, had been killed early one morning while making the day's bread — the old brick ovens had collapsed on him. Unfortunately, only the butcher and a new school remain today, with the addition of a flower shop, a hairdresser, and a dress shop.

Large farms and country houses surround the village. I was born in such a country house, called Yesselcote, which provided me with a sheltered and charming environment to grow up in. There was nothing extraordinary about my childhood, or so I thought at the time. Yesselcote is a large seven-bedroom Victorian house about half a mile from the village. Within the grounds were stables, a tack room, a large brick dog house with pen, a two-car garage with a pit to facilitate the repair of the cars, and a greenhouse, all surrounded by two and a half-acres of well-kept gardens and an orchard. At a later date a tennis court was added.

Our family of seven — two brothers, David and John, two sisters, Jayne and Anita, and my parents — managed to fit into this accommodation quite well, although I had to share a bedroom with John.

With such a large house and grounds, my parents were unable to run everything by themselves, so they hired a gardener, a nanny — whom we very originally called Nanny — and an au pair from Switzerland, whom we replaced each year (the old one presumably being worn out). When the 13th and totally unsatisfactory au pair had gone, my mother opted to have a live in cook during the school holidays.

As children, my siblings and I all had ponies, one for each child. Mine, called Gypsy, was a difficult pony to ride even for the experienced rider. For me the animal was impossible. Although I wasn't keen on riding, the family used to go hunting — a day's exercise I could have done without. Despite my aversion, the pomp and circumstance of the Fox Hunt was glorious. Meeting at the pub, with the "Master of the Hunt" and his team all decked out in their striking red coats, which for some obscure reason are called "Pinks," was a wonderful occasion that brought in crowds of spectators from miles around. The "Whipper In" kept the hounds under close control. There was excitement in the air and horse manure on the ground on those cold winter mornings.

When everybody had indulged in a few drinks, The Master of the Hunt would blow his horn in an exacting manner to signal that we were off. The hounds with the "Whipper In" would lead, then the red-coated huntsmen, followed by the numerous riders and pedestrians. It was a sight, sound, (and smell) to behold. They say that the sound of the hunting horn instills fear into any fox within hearing distance. It certainly instilled fear into me. For you see, I was an awful horseman. I spent the day in fear of falling off — which invariably happened regardless — and by day's end my muscles were sore and my skin rubbed raw from doing it all wrong.

But then, that was only part of it. On my second hunt they caught a fox. I guess that was the idea of it — although I later learned that several members of the hunt obtained their hunting pleasures by participating in extramarital activities in a quiet place within the woods.

This being my first "kill," I was ushered with some excitement to the front of the hunt where I watched in horror as the Huntsman dissected the fox with a small sharp knife and distributed the parts to the "lucky" few. First the tail or "brush," as it was known, followed by the legs, known as the "pads," and finally the prized head. Then, with his hands dripping in fox blood, he smilingly stepped up to me and wiped the blood carefully on my face! This solemn ceremony made me a full-fledged foxhunter.

"How fortunate I feel," I said to myself sarcastically.

Living in the countryside, like anywhere else, has its advantages and disadvantages. On the upside, there were the large, safe areas around our house in which to play, plenty of places to explore, and neighbouring farms to visit on our bikes and ponies. On the down side, there was a distinct lack of friends within walking distance, which sometimes left us feeling a little bored! One such day, my brother John and I — mainly John — noticed that the large Yew hedge that separated the kitchen garden from the more formal garden of our house needed to be trimmed. We had watched the gardener do this in the past, so obviously we knew exactly what to do. Knowing that Dad would be pleased, we asked him if we could cut the hedge, and much to our amazement, he said no, absolutely not. We couldn't believe our ears.

After Dad left for work, John and I discussed the situation and decided that he was just having a bad morning and that he would be delighted and proud if we took the initiative to cut the hedge anyway. So we found two pairs of shears and set about the hedge — at least 8 feet high, 40 feet long, and "A" shaped at the top. John worked on the top section standing on a ladder, while I worked on the lower part of the hedge. It took us nearly all day to trim the hedge and clear up the cuttings. In the end it looked like a job well done.

We anxiously waited for Dad to come home to show him our achievements. We were in for a huge shock and a major lesson in life: he was furious. Absolutely livid. It wasn't that we had cut the hedge, but that we had deliberately disobeyed his orders. As a punishment John was to receive two strokes of the cane, to be administered immediately, and I was given a good telling off. I was told the difference in punishments was due to our age difference — John was nine and I was six — but I still believe it was because I cut my part of the hedge better than he did!

During and after the war almost everything was rationed, or so I was told. With a reasonably large garden at my parent's disposal, it seemed prudent to supplement our food by keeping various animals. We had chickens and bantams (small brown chickens) for both their eggs and meat, and a pig that we kept in a brick pigsty at the bottom of the orchard. He/she was fed with our leftover scraps of food. Our surplus was swapped with friends in the area who kept other livestock.

The chickens and bantams had both a coup and a free-range area and provided us with fresh eggs on a daily basis. It became apparent that we were not the only ones who enjoyed eating chickens — Mr. Fox made several successful attempts at raiding the penned area. I can still hear my father swearing at the fox who had raided the hen house again.

"Enough is enough," he said and decided it was time to sell the remaining chickens. Bromsgrove market day was Thursday; the only problem was how to get our feathered friends there.

After some debate it was decided that the large wicker laundry basket would give the chickens enough air to breathe and keep them in an enclosed environment. With a great deal of complaining by both my father and the chickens, the birds were loaded, one-by-one, into the basket. The leather straps secured the lid of the basket that was then tied down in the open boot of the car. The drive to the market was short, only about five miles. We arrived at the market, an exciting event for me since I had never been to a market where animals were bought and sold. The place was alive with people and animals. Our small black car — with the chickens still strapped to the boot — was somewhat lost in the hubbub of the market place. Dad disappeared to find someone who might be interested in buying our chickens and then reappeared with a businesslike expression on his face, followed by a short, round man with a ruddy well-weathered face.

"Here we are," Dad said, "12 chickens and two bantams."

"Let's take a look at a couple of 'em," said the small man hitching up his britches. My father untied the laundry basket from the boot and placed the eerily quiet basket on the ground. He slowly undid the leather straps and peeked in the basket. There was little movement. With some apprehension, he lifted the lid wide open only to find three chickens moving slightly and the rest appeared dead.

"Oh dear, oh dear, oh me!" said the small man peering inside the basket. "I'm afraid them are no good to no one."

"My god, what the heck happened," Dad muttered, never one to swear in front of children or women.

"You see," said the round man in a knowing way, "when them chickens get in a little space like this," pointing at the laundry basket, "they panic and trample each other to death." Later in life I decided that they might have suffered from carbon monoxide poising from the cars exhaust system. Who knows?

Dad, seeing the hopelessness of the situation, asked the man whether he would take the chickens off his hands. I don't know whether my father had to persuade him with some cash or not, but the outcome when we arrived back home was a dirty, empty laundry basket and no money to show for it.

When my mother asked how things went, he just muttered "Those ruddy chickens!"

CHAPTER 2

SEASIDE SUMMERS

Our family trips to Seaview in the Isle of Wight were always memorable. We invariably went there for the month of August and rented a house. To keep costs down we took as many things as possible with us: linens; blankets; towels; summer clothes for five children, two adults, and the au pair; basic food supplies for as many people, including two sacks of potatoes, a sack of peas, meat, canned food; five bicycles, and so on. It was quite the challenge packing the van, trying to make sure that nothing was missed. My mother and father drove a car each, and we always stopped, en route, for a picnic lunch. The weather always seemed to be perfect, and no matter how much time we gave ourselves we were constantly in a panic to catch the ferry to the island. These were glorious days, except my father was only able to make it for a week or two at the most. Not understanding the demands of running a family business, I always felt short changed.

Seaview is a small village on the northeast shore of the Isle of Wight, an island just off the coast in central southern England. It was, and I believe still is, an excellent seaside town for vacationing. If large fun parks, ample entertainment, and numerous restaurants are your desire, then Seaview is not for you. Seaview vacationers are generally from well-off families from the south of England. Most of them have a love of sailing so the Seaview sailing club is a focal point of activity. Over the years, many, including our family, have purchased homes in the village, which are only frequented in the summer months. This makes owning a business in Seaview very difficult, as it is either "boom" or "bust".

However, Seaview does provide excellent safe and sandy beaches, good sailing, and other boating facilities, all overlooked by a small picturesque village. For the children on holiday there, the greatest allure was the return, each August, of friends made during previous years. Little time was needed to get reacquainted and projects were picked up where they were left off, including minor feuds between the local teenagers and the visiting youth.

As 17-year-old teenagers, we had our driving "wings" and enjoyed going to nearby Ryde. There we experienced the fun parks and ample entertainment. One evening we were returning to Seaview, seven of us in two cars. The agreement was that we would go to Seaview Beach for a walk on this beautiful summer evening. For some reason the two cars became separated and landed at different parking areas to get to the beach, so we set out without the others, only to bump into them a few minutes later. They were mildly excited because they had seen the local youth and felt that they may be looking for a fight. I pooh-poohed the idea and carried on walking along the beach taking in the beautiful night air, not to mention the company.

We weren't walking in a group but were rather straggled out. Suddenly, overpowering the sound of the gently lapping waves, there was an awful commotion and screams from behind us. I spun around to see about 10 local youths arguing and trying to pick a fight. The screams I heard were two of the four girls in our group who wisely had fled the area and gone to hide in some of the beach changing tents. Anita (Neenie) — my younger sister — and another girl stayed behind to try help out and give support. By now we had all gathered in one area and the ring leader was babbling on about something, demanding to know who was driving the car that tried to kill him.

Well, I knew it wasn't my car and told him so in no uncertain terms. For some reason, maybe because I was the most vocal, he was focusing his attention on me. He then lurched forward, grabbed the lapels of my jacket, and all but lifted me off the ground. My brain, numbed a little by a couple of beers, was trying to figure out what I should do about this tricky situation. In a flash it came to me. I brought my arms up high above his and hurled them down hard onto his arms in a karate chop style. To my utter amazement the leader's hands broke away from my coat. A sense of pride welled up inside me as I uttered to myself "I did it, I did it, oh my goodness..."

It was at this exact moment I found out that I was not cut out for the street fighter life. Standing totally still, without flexing at all, I received first a right hook and then a left hook to my face. I dropped like a lead sinker in the sea. Where was my guardian angel?

Spitting sand and blood out of my mouth, I slowly came to my senses while at least six of the locals were kicking me while I was on the ground. I was so enraged that my senses left me for a second time that night. Jumping up from the sand like a missile out of a silo, I let out a maniacal scream of loud expletives that sent all of them scampering. No one was more surprised than I was.

"You cowardly bastards," I screamed at them when I knew it was safe to do so!

Within a minute they disappeared into the dark, frightened that they would be found out. Their parents were all local businessmen that relied heavily on the large influx of visitors in August — an incident of this nature could be very damaging.

We all regrouped and tried to figure out what was going on. It seemed that Claude, the driver of the other car, had come across the locals walking together across the road with their arms linked. As Claude describes it, he had a choice of stopping and probably being mauled by the gang or putting his foot down and hope that they would scatter. He chose the latter, and they did as expected.

The adrenaline rush I had felt during the fight was so great that I failed to realise the pain I was in, until the next morning anyway. My poor, enduring mother packed my swollen face and took me off to a doctor in Ryde who pronounced that my nose was broken in two places. The breaks were bad enough that the good doctor determined that I should have a general anaesthetic when the swelling had gone down so that he could break it again to straighten it out! You would have thought that the two breaks I had already were sufficient. Well, the end result was a straight, if not bumpy nose, so I can't complain.

CHAPTER 3

EARLY SCHOOLING

School — the very word conjures up horrors in my mind. While most children probably dislike school, I can honestly say that I hated every minute of it: the regimentation, the lessons, and the buildings, but not most of the people. My academic record can be described as abysmal at best — a fact about which I am now quite proud, since I found out that Sir Winston Churchill had a similar record.

My first school was Ottalie Hilde School, a private kindergarten and junior school. The owner and principal, Mrs. Hilde, was German and retained her strong accent. The one thing I learned there and can still recall to this day is being able to count to 10 in German.

Graduation from my first formal education was without pomp or circumstance. At the age of seven and a half, I was off to Hillstone School, a boarding preparatory school, in the true English tradition. As my two brothers had been before me, I knew what to expect. If I misbehaved in any way I could expect to be beaten with a cane by the headmaster. Maximum number of strokes, so I was told, was six.

Having brothers there before me was a help in many ways. I got instant respect and name recognition. All children were known by their last name only, so to distinguish between the three Bamfords we were known as Bamford Major, Bamford Minor, and Bamford Minimus. That sounded good to me, but I didn't know how to spell it.

Where my brothers really excelled was in sports. David won the Victor Laudorum award — Latin for "the winner of the games "— for being the best all-round athlete in the school, and John was an exceptional swimmer and rugby football player. I tried exceedingly hard to come up to their standards but failed in the estimation of my coaches. Rugby was a game I enjoyed, even came close to being good, but I was always living under a shadow.

I was big for my age but not particularly strong. Nevertheless, my boxing coach thought I had promise. I was given extra attention, along with a couple of other 12-year-olds. Each year there was a boxing competition between the students, and I was being billed as the next heavyweight champion — just my luck, as I didn't really care for the sport. I learned that if you get hit, it hurts. My match was the last of the competition, and you could cut the tension with a knife, well, my tension at least. My opponent, Plant was his name, a nice chap, and I stepped into the ring. Before I knew it, we had been announced, the bell sounded, and we were sparing. A little jab here, a bigger jab there, when, just before the bell sounded that would end the first round, I managed to land a right hook on Plant's face. I pulled back and saw blood on my glove. It was pouring from his nose. Yuck! The bell rang, thank god, and I went to the corner, not in disgrace this time.

His corner did a remarkable job on his nose (I think they stuffed cotton wool up it), and he came out for the next round. The next two rounds were well thought out by me. My friend Plant was obviously badly hurt and I didn't want to inflict any more damage to his face. I certainly didn't want to get hurt by a blow from Plant. My tactics were set. At the bell, I would come flying out of my corner and spar for a short time and then, before either of us could hurt each other, I would run. This is not easy to do in a ring and had never been practised by me. Plant gave chase and so, as to make the match more exciting, I would quickly turn around and throw a couple more punches. The reaction of the crowd was very surprising; they laughed. In fact they roared. I was quite pleased with myself — I obviously had this fight won. Plant's nose was still bleeding a little, which would surely help the judges make up their mind. I was the better fighter, no doubt about it.

You can imagine my immense surprise and disappointment when the announcement was made and Plant's hand was raised in the air. Totally shattered, more mentally than physically, I took off my boxing gloves for the last time in my life, producing a great feeling of relief. But the internal hurt I felt could not be expressed. I had no idea who was betting on this fight, but they had obviously befriended the judges. Or, maybe this was their first real boxing match. I just hoped they were sprayed in blood. I was pretty upset until it was explained to me that I lost because I was not the aggressor. Even though this was true, there seemed no point in telling my point of view. Anyway, not being the aggressor seemed to be a good trait to me.

CHAPTER 4

MY FATHER

When I was born, my father was 36 and my mother 31, excellent ages for the task they had at hand. Not too young and not too old. It was just after World War II, and my father had been honourably discharged as an "I-don't-know-what" in the Home Guard. This conglomerate of men left in Britain to run the factories, farms, and other essential services formed a nationwide military unit whose basic function was to defend the country from an expected invasion. Just before war broke out, my father had bought a small carpet manufacturing business, Morris & Co., in Kidderminster, the home of carpet manufacturing in Britain. The government commandeered the factory to manufacture webbing for parachute harnesses. Not only did he run the factory during the war, but also he had to carry out Home Guard duty during the evenings and late nights. A German invasion seemed imminent, so this guard duty was serious and no small task, although nothing compared to what the men on the front faced.

With the war over and a large family to feed, my father's focus was on getting the carpet business going, a difficult task indeed in post-war Europe. There were so many shortages after the war; priorities could hardly have included quality carpets. Somehow the business not only survived, but it eventually thrived. He spent many hours working; the only time I really saw him was on Sundays. When I went to boarding school, things were even worse, as then I really only saw him on Sundays during the holiday breaks. However, my most enjoyable memories of my father were the moments we spent together touring the factory. It seemed to me that all the weavers, maintenance personnel, office staff, and general factory workers admired him and took pride in what they were doing. I loved the rhythmic sounds of the looms, the smell of yarn and jute in the sheds, and the general happiness that most of his employees displayed.

People talk about my father in superlatives, with glowing terms filled with love, affection, and sorrow. It is a great pity that I never really knew him. He died at the age of 50, when everything in his life was coming to fruition. Morris & Co. was growing in sales and profit, and I am sure he was proud of the manner in which his family was growing and maturing. He was on the Board of Governors at Hillstone School and would have gone on to carry out many other charitable and voluntary works.

Our nervous House Master at Ellesmere, my new school, told John and me of his death. I suspected that something was going on, but I never really knew. In those days, that was the way it was done. Details of a patient's illness were kept from the patient and to some degree the family. Certainly no information was given to the children. The only information I gained was by overhearing conversations that were not intended for my ears and by keen observations. I knew that he died of cancer, but to this day I don't even know with certainty what type. It seemed to me that he suffered a great deal of pain and was very thin. The last time I saw him was when I left home for my first term at Ellesmere College, aged 13. He was standing in the hall with his hands in the hollow of his back, and as I went through the front door I waved good-bye. He said something about working hard and being good and that was that. Hugs and kisses were not the norm in those days, not for boys. No, that would be a sign of weakness, of femininity. I never considered it an issue, especially when I think that my father had to call his father "sir".

Who can imagine what horrors were going through his mind as John and I departed? He must have known that he had little time left, and the likelihood of him not seeing us again was very real. My mother said good-bye to us on the driveway as the factory chauffeur drove us the 60 miles to school.

The same horrific situation must have occurred when he saw my sisters, Jayne and Neenie, off to their separate boarding schools. David, my eldest brother, had completed his public school[1] education at Uppingham and was now studying at a technical college and working at the family factory. His presence must have been a great comfort to my mother.

The family gathered for the funeral. David came to fetch John and me from Ellesmere in my father's Jaguar XK150 — a wonderful automobile that my father had purchased new six months earlier when he felt he was getting well again. We drove home fast and furiously. Not much was said; there was no need for talk and empty words. Sitting in the middle, on the hump, I was too busy holding on to talk. Anyway, I was the quiet one, a person of few words. My feelings were strong, but words were few — the English way. Internally everyone was grieving, but you would never know it. I never saw a tear shed but knew that everyone cried.

My father was a person who appeared to be loved by everyone: family, friends, business associates, and employees. The night before the funeral, after much persuasion by me, it was decided that I could attend the funeral service, but not the cremation. Neenie, aged 12, was considered too young and was not allowed to attend either which, in retrospect, was made with the best of intentions but was the wrong decision. She missed the chance of feeling what I felt.

Dad's funeral was one of the proudest days of my life. The village church in Chaddesley Corbett, a reasonably sized church with approximately 250 seats, was filled to capacity and people were even standing at the back of

---

1. Public schools in England are private schools for 13-18 year olds, normally a boarding school.

the church and spilling to the outside. There were mourners there from every walk of life; some I knew, many I didn't, but all were there to pay their last respects to my father. I was very proud of him and all of his achievements that had been made in a short lifetime.

After four days, I returned to face the continuous monotony and drudgery of everyday life at school. Few people noticed that I had been away and fewer yet knew why. That was fine with me. I wasn't looking for pity anyway. Even though none of the masters said anything to me, I felt certain they knew. They were unnaturally kind. They never raised their voice at me, only asked me questions that they felt sure I could answer or better still never asked me a question at all. Unfortunately, this lasted only a short time, but I was grateful for the reprieve.

CHAPTER 5

A CHANGE

Until fairly recently boarding schools were purposely unisex. All of the pupils and 95 percent of the faculty and staff at Hillstone and Ellesmere were male. This didn't sit well with me. Obviously, with changing hormones the more mature boys were hankering after the opposite sex, and some went to extraordinary lengths to satisfy their needs. This was certainly true for me in my last two years at Ellesmere, but there were other reasons I hated being in such a masculine environment. It had to do with my physical state, which I needed to change. Who wants to change? Maybe the young want to be older or the old want to look younger, but whether you want it or not, change is always occurring; it is inevitable, as inevitable as death itself. But real change, dramatic change can only occur with the help of others. And that is what I sought. A dramatic change. It's not something that I dreamed up or even something that evolved over the last few years. No, it was something that I had thought about, dreamed about since a very early age, as a 4-or maybe 5-year-old at the latest.

I really don't remember my age — it is irrelevant anyway; the change I dreamed of was not possible. It wasn't possible physically, and more than that, it wasn't possible socially. Who had ever heard of a boy wanting to be a girl? Totally ridiculous. A sissy. There must be something wrong with him. But all the same, the idea, the feelings, the longing, the overwhelming desires never left me.

Of course, I never told anyone about these feelings of mine. I would have been humiliated, rejected, thought to be insane. No, it was the 1950s; this was my secret, and I just needed to forget about it, do what I was supposed to do, what others wanted and expected me to do. And that is what I did.

Except I couldn't forget about it. Every single day I thought about it and wondered what I should do and every single day I did what was expected of me and life went on.

Outwardly, I appeared as normal as any other boy. I tried my best to follow in my brother's footsteps. Anything that appeared girlish or feminine I rejected, overcompensating for fear of my secret being discovered. But then feelings can be very strong. And when the feelings became overwhelming, I would go to my mother's or sister's rooms and try to make myself look as female as possible. In a family of five children, nannies, au pairs etc. it was difficult to get time alone but somehow I managed it. I became an expert at putting everything back exactly as I found it, always in fear of being discovered. My early focus on this type of detail, I believe, led to my excellent eye for physical detail in later life.

Boarding school was an impossible place to act on any feminine feelings. One day, while at Hillstone, around the age of 10 or 11, there was a newspaper article that caught my eye: "Man has sex change operation." My heart started pounding as I read about a Frenchman, now known as Coccinelle. He underwent a sex change operation in Casablanca, Morocco and now had a vagina and was working as an actress and entertainer in Paris. He had always felt that he was a woman, and no attempt at suppressing these feelings worked. As a man, he was suicidal, had been to numerous psychiatrists, was subjected to electric shock treatment but nothing had worked.

As young schoolboys, we had crowded around the newspaper that was attached to a slanted board, affixed to the wall so that several people could read the paper at the same time. We joked and giggled about the article that seemed so silly to them. But I was transfixed. Here was someone else, someone who had feelings like mine. I wasn't alone after all. And there was an operation available — I could be female. This was incredible, and my situation suddenly did not seem so hopeless. But then the realization began to creep in that it was highly unlikely I could ever do such a thing. For one my family would not allow it — there was an honor to uphold. I had never been to any psychiatrist and wasn't suicidal, and I certainly didn't want any electric shock treatment. No, this couldn't happen to me. Our situations weren't so similar after all. I tried to put any such thoughts behind me.

The early teenage years were particularly hard for me. My voice broke. My facial hair was coming in thick and fast, and as my hair was jet black, I soon developed a shadow. I thought that any hope of becoming a female was gone. Then there were all the sports I was involved in at Ellesmere and there were a lot: rugby, swimming, track and field events, tennis, squash, water polo, and sailing. Afternoons spent at the sailing club on one of the meres[2] was a wonderful respite for me. During the week, there was never anyone else there, so I had the clubhouse to myself. I could do whatever, be whatever I wanted, including being the female I so desperately felt that I was.

My body was changing shape, and my physique was now very masculine. Although I didn't think so at the time — like most teenagers — I was a pretty good-looking youngster, and the girls were showing a lot of interest in me. I was happy to respond, to experiment and date, as many boys in my age group did. I didn't have any homosexual feelings. The guys to me were buddies to hang out with. At a "boys only" boarding school it becomes very obvious who is gay, both to the boys and the teachers. Homosexual activity was not tolerated by the school and was reason for instant expulsion, but it was still going on. Generally speaking, the boys were rarely taunted and were guardedly accepted into the community, but they certainly could not be open about it — just as I couldn't be open about my situation.

---

2. A mere is a small lake

PART 2
TEEN YEARS

CHAPTER 6

ELLESMERE COLLEGE

As we turned the corner into the private driveway of Ellesmere College for the first time, I had a lump in my throat and a knot in my stomach, probably no different from any other new boy arriving for the school year. We passed the rugby fields on the drive in, and as we rounded the corner I saw the building where I would be spending a good deal of my life for the next five years. I say building because that basically was it: one huge, red brick building that was three stories high and in the shape of a double cross ‡. Of course, over the years extensive additions were made. The building was very foreboding, stark and rather prison-like in appearance. There were few plants, shrubs, or flowers surrounding it, but there was plenty of grass. John pointed out the rugby fields, the first XI cricket pitch, swimming pool, and gym on the way to the front door. Saying good-bye to my parents at home was probably a good thing. There were plenty of new boys arriving who were having a much tougher time of it than me, and I was lucky to have John to chaperone me for the first few days.

Life at Ellesmere College was mostly boring, punctuated with moments of excitement that were always clouded with the inevitable stressful classroom lessons and tests. I dreaded every moment spent on academia, and my term reports and class placing reflected it. There were always words of encouragement from home when I managed to lift myself from bottom place. My great saviour, however, was my brother John who could be relied upon to always bring home a report a couple of notches worse than mine.

A boy's first year at Ellesmere guaranteed him a place in New Dorm, a 50-bed dormitory run by four senior boys. The Dorm Prefects had the privilege of flogging the new boys with a hard slipper at will. The more sadistic prefects did it often and for the pettiest of crimes. Fortunately, in my year we had fairly reasonable prefects. My second term at school I was made a monitor, who helped manage the dorm for the Prefects. I am sure this appointment was made to take my mind off my father's death, but it had its benefits: this is when I started developing management skills that I would constantly use in the future. Apparently I was pretty good at it because a couple of years later, and much to my surprise, I had the dubious honour of being a Dorm Prefect.

One night, I was strolling around the three rows of beds in this large dormitory as everyone was getting ready for bed when, without cause, a poster of the Beatles fell off the wall. The Beatles at that time were all the rage, especially at Ellesmere, as many of the boys came from the Liverpool area. Some of the boys came back talking about visiting the Cavern and hearing the Beatles on the school holiday, which meant nothing to me at the time. The early 60s were a great time for music. Many fledgling groups started to appear in the clubs and went on to become the biggest names in the music industry. We had many arguments as to who was better: the Beatles or the Rolling Stones. I favoured the Beatles, even sporting a mild version of a Beatles haircut!

Referring to the Beatles poster, I jokingly said, "Oh, something terrible will happen tonight." Not in a thousand years was I prepared for what was about to happen.

It was about 6:30 in the morning when a boy from another house raced into our dormitory, jumped onto my bed, and looked out of the window. His legs were shaking furiously.

"What the fuck was going on here last night?" he demanded accusingly.

"What the hell are you babbling about?" I said sleepily. I have never been very coherent first thing in the morning.

"Look! There's somebody lying on the ground down there. Can you see him down there?" he said, jabbing his finger at the window. Dave Howell, the dorm captain, and I strained our necks and sure enough there was the body of a boy four floors down, directly beneath our bathroom windows. It was so surreal I didn't quite know what to say or do.

The three of us ran to the bathroom area and again we were asked accusingly whether we had had a wild party last night.

"No!" David and I said in unison rather upset by the accusation.

The bathroom had four bathtubs split with two bathroom stalls. When we arrived, we found one of the two stall doors locked and no one in it. The bathroom windows in both stalls were wide open. So, we concluded, the poor kid either went to the toilet, locked the door, and purposely jumped to his death or was playing a prank and tried to climb out of one window and into the other one but lost his footing and fell to his death. Either way, the whole episode was a terrible incident and questions were quickly directed at the four of us in charge. The police soon ruled out foul play, but I don't think the coroner could decide whether the incident was an accident or suicide.

The school handled the incident professionally and there was little to no bad publicity in any of the media, and school life was back to normal in a couple of days. As a parent today, I cannot imagine how the boy's parents must have felt.

Being injured was bad enough, but visiting Matron could be even more painful, both mentally and physically. I know that somewhere inside there was a soft spot, but normally she was as tough as an old boot. If you felt that you needed medical attention, you had to silently line join the line in the corridor outside her surgery after breakfast.

"What's the matter with you?" she would say to the first boy in the line.

"I don't feel well," the uninitiated boy would say. All the others would wince knowing that was the worst answer he could have given.

"Stand up straight and put your shoulders back," she barked as the rest of the boys in the line cringed, remembering their experience with this routine.

"Now what's the matter with you?" Matron repeated.

"I don't feel well," the terrified boy would say again quietly.

"I know you don't feel well. No boy in this line feels well — that's why you are all here. None of you boys feel well do you?"

A mixture of "yes Matron" and "no Matron" came from the line. The yes Matron boys were thinking, yes you are right, and the no Matron boys were thinking, no I don't feel well.

"You are all pathetic," she would mandate as she passed onto the next boy — this time it was me.

"What's the matter with you, Bamford," she said with a slight smile. I think she quite liked me for some reason. Or maybe it was just because I was already standing up straight with my shoulders back.

"I have sprained a muscle in my back, Matron."

"How do you know you have sprained a muscle? You don't have any medical training, do you Bamford?" She continued, "If you hurt your back so much you wouldn't be standing there with your shoulders so far back, would you?"

"No Matron."

That was a fairly painless interrogation I thought as she passed onto the next boy.

Once in the surgery, she announced that I sprained a muscle in my back and that I would get a massage of an ointment that I had not heard of before. She was very thorough giving the area a good deep rub for several minutes.

"You are done Bamford," she said with a smile giving me a hard slap on my back.

"Thank you, Matron," I said getting dressed, feeling genuinely pleased that she had given me a good and thorough massage.

It wasn't until I reached the end of the corridor before entering the lobby that I began to feel it. At first it was a tingling sensation that quickly turned into a burning sensation and then my back felt like it was on fire.

Oh my God this hurts like hell. Matron's put the wrong cream on my back! I quickly turned and went back to the surgery.

"What do you want Bamford?" she asked sternly.

"My back is burning like anything."

"Good, it is supposed to. Get out of my way!" she uttered, brushing passed me.

I reiterated my story to my friends who were most unimpressed.

"Oh Matron rubbed in some 'Hell Fire' and gave you a slap on the back, did she? That's the normal treatment for muscle aches and pains — Matron loves to prescribe it," my friend said, adding that it was actually pretty good stuff.

School was a living nightmare between the stress of poor classroom performance, the continuous threat of being flogged — especially in the early years — and the long stretches of boredom that were exaggerated by the fact that we were rarely allowed outside the school grounds. Playing rugby in the winter terms and sailing on the meres during the summer term offset the boredom a little, but not by much.

It seemed that life was purposely made unpleasant with 'nice' little touches: cold water only in the dormitories, the school toilets being placed outside with no doors, two hours of evening prep work in a huge hall sitting four to a bench three rows deep. All very Dickensian.

Although I can say with absolute certainty that there was no year that came close to being enjoyable, it seemed that with each passing year school life became a little more bearable. Part of the improvement had to do with a change of headmaster my second year. The school was part of the Woodard Foundation and over the past 100 years or so had always appointed a clergyman to the headmaster position. I imagine this was done to ensure that we had a good religious upbringing in the Church of England, which included daily compulsory services in the school chapel — twice on Sundays — and a solid dose of Divinity classes.

The new headmaster was quite different from all the old ones. As a 29-year-old former captain of England's touring rugby team, he brought a sense of vigour and youthfulness that had been missing with the previous headmasters — all older clergy members. He gradually eased up on the rules, outlawed floggings by any boys except the Captain of School, allowed bicycles, and eased up on the uniform requirements. New rules withstanding, I still resented being there.

In my last year, there was a self-made respite to the drudgery. I had a group of friends who were creative and somewhat carefree. One day, two of them approached me and said they had recently been on a bike ride and come across a car in a small garage that was in good working order. The owner of the garage said that the sale price was £20, but to them he would sell it for £15, or $20 at today's exchange rate!

"You are joking," I said in disbelief. "A working car for £15!"

My mind began racing, thinking of all the possibilities that a set of wheels would bring me, err I mean us.

"Are you in?" asked one of my anxious buddies.

"Well" I said pensively. "It sounds pretty good to me but I can't imagine what sort of car £15 would buy. Who gets to use it when. What about the running cost?"

"Come on Bamford, are you in or not? If you're not in then you can't use it," the other one said impatiently, in the usual public-school, high-pressure sales approach.

"OK let's go and have a look at it." I said, semi-excitedly to buy some extra time.

The whole idea sounded very appealing, but too good to be true. I thought about going to neighbouring towns: Shrewsbury, Whitchurch, Oswestry, or even Llangollen, nestled in the beautiful Welsh countryside. I thought about meeting different people, visiting the pubs, and just smelling the air of freedom.

I also thought about the car breaking down miles from school or getting into an accident and wondered where in the world we were going to keep it. Nobody had thought of that minor issue! All of these thoughts might be irrelevant if the car was a load of scrap and for £15 one couldn't really expect much else.

The three of us arrived at the small corner garage. It was a bright, sunny afternoon, with the air full of excitement. There were only a handful of cars for sale, and I quickly scanned the grassy lot to try and locate the car my friends were talking about. Then my eyes focused on a beautiful navy-coloured Ford Pilot V8, probably manufactured in the late 40s.

"Hey! Look at this one," I said jokingly, "This must be the one."

To my utter amazement, they both confirmed.

I stood there dumbfounded. "Are you sure this is the car?" I asked. "It looks far too good to be worth just £15." There was little to no rust on the body, although the paintwork was somewhat dull. The upholstery was in reasonable condition, if not a little dirty. Some of the stitching had come loose but nothing to be concerned about. As I sat in the front passenger seat appraising the interior, one of my friends jumped into the driver's seat and with a big smile.

"Hey, look at this Bamford." He proceeded to pull on a cord located at the top of the driver's side window and blinds started covering the back windows. What an amazing mechanism, what an amazing idea — perfect for a 17-year-old.

I was shown the steering wheel lock feature: it was operated by a key and the ignition was turned on and off with a toggle switch. The car also had an automatic jack system, meaning that all four wheels could come off the ground just by turning a lever in the engine compartment. I had never seen anything like it before or since. It had that beautiful sound that only a V8, or in this case a V7, can make. I was sold. Quite incredible and all for just £15.

The salesman was a nice enough man, although I was instinctively suspicious of him as I am of all salesmen. All the bargaining had been done before my arrival, and all that was left was to pay £5 each.

I had my money out of my wallet in a flash. The other two stood motionless.

"What's the problem?" I said in a concerned voice.

The one friend mumbled that he hadn't got any money but was expecting his parents to send him £10 very shortly.

"Same with me," the other one said with a nervous laugh. Now the salesman started looking anxious and somewhat irritated.

"I can't save this car for you for long, you know. There is another gentleman interested in buying it."

We all knew full well that there was no one else, but the statement had the desired effect. All of us wanted the car, and we weren't about to lose it, even to an imaginary person. This car was my ticket to freedom, fun, and frolicking. I had a £20 note in my wallet, which I dutifully handed over to the salesman. A few minutes later we had the logbook in hand and the car was mine.

Since I was the sole owner of the car, I had the privilege of driving it back to school. It didn't occur to me until much later that the vehicle was neither taxed nor insured. Even when I realised it and fully intended to do something about it, I never did. Such is the irresponsibility of youth.

It was quite a large car, so we were able to stack at least two of the bikes in the boot. On the trip back to school, after the initial ecstasy had worn off a little, it started to dawn on us that the gearbox was making a bit of a grinding noise. In the stress and excitement of purchasing the car, we had forgotten to road test it. Too late now: we were comfortably moving back to school at a relatively fast speed, compared to the bikes anyway, and we knew full well that there wasn't any warranty on this car. Cars were strictly forbidden on school grounds, so we parked it out of sight at a farmyard that was near the school.

Word of the grand purchase soon spread among my circle of close-knit friends. Of course, they all wanted to see it, so we traipsed out to the farmyard again, trying to look as inconspicuous as possible. This was hard on an open driveway about a third of a mile long.

When the gang saw it, they were incredulous. They too could see all sorts of possibilities and were anxious to compare diary dates with me.

"Wednesday evening," one of them announced, "Susan has a small party that she insists I attend."

The obvious problem had already started to rear its head: everyone was going to request the car for every party and event in town. I immediately made it clear that they were welcome to accompany me on any trip, but that no one was going to take the car out on their own. Unless, that is, they were prepared to pay for their share of ownership. Surprisingly, no one uttered a sound of complaint or offered to pay for their share of the car.

The decision to keep a car at school quickly proved positive, although I had to be extremely careful how and, more importantly, when I used it. Shrewsbury was a reasonably large town some 20 miles from Ellesmere and had the obvious attractions for a teenager. My new girlfriend, Suzanne, lived in Shrewsbury, and for Saturday night parties there was an understandable draw, although somewhat risky. I recall one night the car ran out of petrol on my way to Shrewsbury. A feeling of despair came over me, as I was a long way from school and was concerned about hitching a ride in case one of the Masters saw me. Unlikely, I know, but still a large enough concern that motivated me not to do it.

A more unlikely situation, or actually, the most unlikely situation, occurred instead. A school friend whose parents had allowed him to have their car for the weekend was driving on the same road and recognising my car, stopped to see if I needed any assistance. Although I knew I had a "guardian angel" that had been watching over me for some time now, this was the point when I knew the angel was hard at work on my behalf. It turned out that my friend was bound for the same party!

This late in my school career, friendships were strong and one of the strongest was with Peter Laing. He lived in Birmingham, close to my hometown, and had a great sense of humour. His smoking habit was notorious — in his last year the headmaster allowed him to go to his house to smoke rather than allow him to smoke in front of other students.

His parents bought a small cottage near the school so they could visit on weekends. The Laings had three sons educated at Ellesmere, Peter being the middle one. Peter's father watched almost every home rugby game and since Peter and I were in the same team, I became well acquainted with his father. The cottage was in easy cycling distance, so Peter and I would go there often. He also had a Vespa scooter which increased our range and danger limit. Fortunately, the scooter had a low top speed since Pete was not a slow driver. It was exhilarating riding through the winding and high-sided lanes in Shropshire.

We often used the cottage as a base for our outings in town. I met my new girlfriend Suzanne there several times and frequently went to the local pub. The kind, friendly publican had to let us in through the back door since we were not yet 18, the legal drinking age.

Like most any teenager, after living with the rules at Ellesmere for a short time I learned the ropes and found creative ways to circumvent the tedium and chores. One of the more favoured and legal methods was to volunteer for the school marching band. Not only was it somewhat enjoyable, but more importantly, it relieved one from obligatory duty in the CCF (the Combined Cadet Force), a training cadet corps for the army. I can't remember what other privileges it brought, but I know it was well worth the practice time required by the band.

My brother John was in the band as a side drummer. His drumming skills were never questioned, and he rose in rank to become the lead drummer — the silver drummer. Of course, I wanted to follow in his footsteps, so when I applied to join the band I wanted to be a side drummer.

"No drummer spots available came the reply." What were they trying to tell me?

"OK," I said to the Sergeant Major, who ran the band, "I would like to be a bugler."

"Out of bugles," came back the reply, "but the cymbal position is open."

"Cymbals!" I said, "But you don't need any skills for those."

"Exactly" said the Sergeant Major, who up until this point in time I had rather liked.

"It's not that bad, Bamford," said one of my friends, "at least you will get to wear all the decorative paraphernalia on parade days." This included a real leopard skin, a white leather sash, white gloves, and a white belt with brass buckle and white gaiters. The base drummer, tenor drummers, and the cymbal player were the only members who wore this uniform, drawing the envy of everyone else.

"And you will be the lead cymbal player," he added thoughtfully, knowing that there was only one in the band.

Knowing that the alternative was not to be in the band at all, I agreed to the assignment.

The music was very simple, and it didn't take me long to become proficient at my instrument — although there is more to it than meets the eye. At least I can honestly say that I never played an incorrect note!

The whole band was coming together well and was focused on an important public appearance at Remembrance Sunday, an annual event in November where the whole school attended church in Ellesmere with the rest of the town's people to remember the dead of the two world wars. The school's CCF, Boy Scouts, and the band attended in uniform, and after the service we paraded through the streets of Ellesmere back to school. This event was taken very seriously and was always attended by a senior ranking army officer to take the salute.

It was a beautiful, crisp late autumn day as we all congregated around the war memorial and heard a bugler blow The Last Post. It is invariably a moving moment, even for a 17-year-old. We then all formed our positions for the march, with the band leading the way. We were a sight to behold with all our instruments sparkling in the sun and our whites looking whiter than ever. On command, we marched off playing the routine we had practised for so long. We were playing at our peak and the crowds that lined the streets really appreciated us. This year we were very fortunate, so we were told, because we had a general present to take the salute. As we approached the podium, we were given the order eyes right (you can't actually salute) and there was the general, immaculately dressed, saluting back. The music was on beat.

Bang, bang, bang went the drums. Bang, bang, thud, crash went the cymbals!

What in hell is going on, I thought, as I quickly turned and un-saluted. Oh my God! My heart stopped and my mind raced. A quick review determined that I had a cymbal in my left hand and a white leather strap in my right with no cymbal attached. The thud was my right hand hitting the left cymbal, the crash was the right cymbal hitting the street and rolling through all the legs of the marching band along the side of the road until it came to rest in the gutter with the curved side up.

The gasps from the excited onlookers could not be heard over the band, but the shock could be seen on their faces. My stomach knotted as I was faced with a major dilemma: stay in rank and continue marching as prescribed by military decorum or break rank and pick up the cymbal as was prescribed by the school purser's decorum? A quick review of the situation revealed to me that since I was eating, breathing, and living school every day it was better for me to retrieve the cymbal — not an easy task.

I was on the right-hand side of the line-up, and the cymbal had somehow made its way over to the left-hand gutter. I stopped marching and tried moving forwards and sideways at the same time, squeezing myself between the double bass drum and the side drummers in front of us. It was not hard to locate the shiny cymbal lying like an upside down plate. I bent down to pick it up, but found that with my thick white leather gloves that this was next to impossible. I couldn't get my fingers underneath the damn thing to grab it, and much to the further amusement of the crowd, I found myself pushing the cymbal along the street, causing more damage to this delicate musical instrument. Finally, I came to my senses and took off my gloves and picked up the wretched thing and reversed my dance back into my position in the band. For the 20-minute march back to school, I felt a little stupid not being able to play my instrument. Personally, I thought that the music didn't sound the same without the cymbals, although most people told me they didn't notice the difference.

One of my true escapes from school life was sailing. The school had a sailing club, and we sailed 14-foot dinghies on a mere near the school. It wasn't a very large mere but big enough to sail, race, and have fun. The town had a sailing club that we were allowed to use. The school encouraged sailing as an activity and allowed boys to keep their own sailing dinghies there, which I did. My boat was one my father, a keen sailor, had built at his factory from a kit. We had competitive sailing events against a few other schools that also had the privilege of a school sailing club.

There was one such school, H.M.S. Conway, located on the island of Angelsey in North Wales, which, as the name implies, was a naval school. Until a few years prior, the school was actually located on an old, three-masted wooden ship — the naval cadets literally learned the ropes. That came to an end when the ship went up in smoke. However, their seamanship was never to be questioned. A sailing match against H.M.S. Conway was always intimidating. As our rather scruffy team turned up in a very old charabanc, the most impeccably dressed naval cadets in uniform met us. The boats we were sailing were old and heavy — nothing like the boats that we were used to. In a pre-match briefing we were told of the very strong tidal current that flowed through the Menai Straights, the water separating Angelsey from the mainland. This current at its peak ran at about six knots. Needless to say our efforts were pitiful, and most of us ended up at least a mile downstream from the starting line before we had even figured out which rope worked what. The school's safety launch, manned by some very stiff "nose in the air" type naval personnel, chased after us to tow us back to the start line. All very discouraging. However, we did beat them once on our own mere where there were neither currents nor wind. I hate to think what happened to them when they returned to their ship.

When I left Ellesmere, my boat was beginning to show signs of wear, so we decided to donate it to the school's sailing club. I felt very good about that. I am sure many students were able to derive the same enjoyment out of her as I had done.

CHAPTER 7

LATE TEENS

My father died in October 1960, and although his imminent demise had been known for some time, it was only about eight weeks earlier that his affairs been put in order, especially in regards to the carpet factory. Our family was very fortunate to have some bright legal and financial advisors to help us through the nightmare of minimising estate duties and resolving succession issues at the factory. At the age of 20, it was obvious that my eldest brother, David, was not experienced enough in carpet manufacturing or business management to take over.

Since my mother now controlled a vast majority of the stock, either in her own name or in trusts, she was the obvious and only choice to become the Chairman and Managing Director at the age of 45. As one of the first female chairmen, it was decided that she should be known as Madam Chairman. With five children ranging in age from 12 to 20, with four still at boarding school, she certainly had her work cut out.

First she had to win over the senior management team, all of whom, I am sure, felt that they should be playing a larger role than they were. Then my father's only brother, Arthur, a manufacturer's representative in the London area, strongly felt that he should have a major role to play. Plus, there were some 300 employees, all concerned about their future employment prospects. All these were very real issues that had to be dealt with, and she managed it all with grace, good advice, and courage.

I am sure it was not all easy sailing and that the usual problems of running a family business were forever presenting themselves, but overall the business flourished and expanded.

Upon leaving Ellesmere in the summer of 1961, John joined the family business in the manner that my father had envisioned. He saw David as the Managing Director, John as the Director of Facilities, and myself as Director of Finance. This just left me to finish my schooling, estimated to be in 1965, and then all three brothers would be in the business. As it turned out, my mother had higher goals for me than that. She felt, if I put my mind to it, that I could become a Chartered Accountant. With this qualification, I would always be employable and would be able to find a good job, but it also meant another five years of studying and working at a professional accounting firm.

With no better ideas of my own, a career in accounting seemed appropriate. My mother had several contacts with accounting firms through her financial advisors at the factory, and we were put in touch with a small accounting firm, Foster & Stephens, in Birmingham. It was decided that a small accounting firm would be better than a large one because I was more likely to have broader experience across all departments. After several interviews, it was agreed that I would become an "articled clerk" through the Institute of Chartered Accountants in England and Wales, with a payment to the firm of £900. This money was to be refunded as I successfully progressed through my studies, receiving a third when I passed my intermediate exams, another third when I passed part one of my finals, and the remaining third when I fully qualified. Officially, the money helped the firm fund my education, but in reality it seemed to be a way to keep the "riffraff" out. My annual salary was set at £400 a year, which amounted to $7-6s-8d[3] a week, just enough to buy a couple of rounds at the pub.

---

3. 7 pounds, 6 shillings and 8 pence

I can't say that I enjoyed the work — most of the time I was unchallenged and bored. However, there were two benefits that I received at Foster & Stephens that I always greatly appreciated, although I can't say that they had much to do with the company itself: the annual Christmas brandy presented to all staff members by the senior partner and luncheon vouchers that could be used at local pubs and restaurants. Invariably, each lunch time, we would go to a pub and have a sandwich and a couple of pints of beer. I don't know how we did it, as I know for sure, that today I would be asleep by mid-afternoon. Maybe I was and nobody noticed.

In retrospect, I don't think my mother ever received the recognition she deserved for running the family business. She had taken over as my father was dying, successfully ran it for eight years, took the company public, and eventually agreed to sell it for an excellent price. Granted, she had her advisors to help her through all the pitfalls of running a business, but so do all successful companies. She was firm and fair, well-respected by the sales representatives and other employees, and had a good eye for carpet design and marketing.

I have many wonderful memories of the factory: the ear-deafening, rhythmic noise of the looms hard at work, the smell of the jute and yarn, the genuinely friendly smiles of all the people who worked there. From the age of 13 until it was sold, the "Works" as it was fondly known in our family, became a large playground. In the early years after my father's death, John and I spent many hours "helping" the employees with their work. We learned how to run the yarn stock room, run a loom on a rudimentary level, work all the machines in the machine shop, and drive the vans and the fork lift trucks. There was hardly a corner we didn't get into.

Most boys in their teenage years enjoy tinkering around with mechanical things, and John and I were no exception. We were fortunate to have the factory and all of its amenities at our disposal. John was a brilliant self-taught mechanic. To him, things came apart in a very orderly manner and then went back together again with amazing ease, coupled with a few choice and well-timed swear words.

Sometimes it was hard to find a project to work on, but on one particular day John came across a small hill climb car needing some loving care and attention. This car was a two-seater, with no roof and just a couple of small windscreens in front of each seat. It lacked any safety features such as an anti-roll bar or seat belts. Instead of doors, the sides were lowered a little so that one could jump over the side to get in. Built for going over rough ground, it had quite good acceleration but was not that fast. In other words, it was a perfect project for John and me.

A good friend of David's owned the car, but it took us some time and a lot of pestering to persuade him to allow us to "improve the vehicle." I was never quite sure whether we had his full permission, but next thing I knew it was at the Works in many pieces! Working together we not only managed to repair it, but it was also somewhat improved.

Sundays at the factory were always very quiet — it was the only day of the week it was closed. One Sunday, all three of us — David, John, and myself — were there messing around with the car. David had persuaded us to let him drive it, and I was in my usual seat when he came up with a terrific idea.

"Let's see how fast we can get this thing to go," he said with smile.

"All right," I replied with some trepidation, knowing that David was not John when it came to mechanical skills or driving ability.

So we drove up to the end of the concrete driveway and turned the car around at the entrance gate. With grim determination, David stuck his tongue in his cheek, a lifelong habit, and floored the accelerator. I was momentarily pushed back into my seat as we quickly accelerated, then the speed levelled off at 30 miles per hour. At the bottom of the driveway, the road took a sharp turn to the right and then a sharp turn to the left. I was a little anxious as we approached the corner, as I didn't know whether David was going to slow down or how the car would handle the turn. I soon had my answers: David wasn't going to slow down and the car handled the sharp turn terribly. As we maneuvered the corners, the car become unstable, and I could feel the passenger side lifting off the ground as we rounded the second corner. That sudden feeling of panic came over me as we started to roll over. It all seemed like things were moving in slow motion, and I had a decision to make: was it better for me to stay in the car or jump out? Without a roof or any protection if I chose to stay in the car, I decided to jump. By this time, we were no longer going 30 miles an hour, but we were definitely going fast enough to get badly hurt. John was on the side, away from the road, watching the whole thing in horror. David had no choice: he was on the bottom side of the car, stuck behind the steering wheel.

I've heard that in life-threatening moments like these, the shock takes over, and you feel no pain. That's a complete lie: the pain was bloody excruciating! I landed on the ground, face down, and kept sliding along. My clothes were ripped, and my legs, knees, elbows, arms, and chin were all badly grazed, but nothing appeared broken or permanently damaged. David was grazed and bruised as well, but considering what could have happened we were extremely lucky, and we knew it.

We spent the next hour or so cleaning up the best we could and deciding how to tell our mother. In the end, the decision was to downplay the whole event, if asked, but to try and avoid the confrontation altogether. We sneaked into the house, a fairly easy task, and changed out of our torn clothes. Everything was going according to plan until I was getting ready for bed. Suddenly, my mother appeared on the scene, with me in my underwear, and gasped when she saw the grazes and bruising on my body.

"What on earth have you done to yourself," she said anxiously?

Trying to think quickly, the best I could come with was that I had tripped while running at the factory.

"Oh!" she said, "It must have been a nasty fall, are you all right?"

I didn't expect her to believe me, but she didn't question me further. A mother's intuition, I guess.

CHAPTER 8

WELL-EARNED HOLIDAYS

The friendships I made at Ellesmere College were strong. During the last couple of months at school, plans had been formalised for four of us to have some well-earned R&R on the Adriatic coast in Italy. By that time, I was the proud owner of a new Austin Mini (insured, taxed and very legitimate this time), and Alastair owned or had the use of a Hillman Imp. Both cars were extremely small, even by European standards. However, I always considered my car superior since the Hillman had an engine in the rear and was made of aluminium, so it was very light and a little unpredictable.

The plan was for Pete and me to travel in the Mini and Alastair and Phil to travel in the Imp. We travelled to the South of France without incident, arriving early in the morning. We had a lazy day on the public beach in the exclusive Juan les Pins area and a good, but cheap meal — it mainly consisted of bread and wine — before leaving for the East Coast of Italy. By our reckoning, the drive would take about 12 hours, so we would arrive early in the morning. This strategy, we thought, would maximise our daylight vacation time and get us to our destination, Riccione, early.

We set out a little more inebriated than we should have been but not quite drunk. We drove, in convoy, through the night, switching drivers regularly. By 9 a.m. we were a little over half way there! We trudged on, determined to get to our destination by nightfall. It was stupid and dangerous. I clearly remember waking up to a terrible clattering of stones against the underside of the car. I wondered what the hell Pete was up to before I suddenly realised that I was the one who was driving!

We arrived in Riccione around 3 p.m. and started to look for a suitable campground. All the listed campgrounds were full, which was only natural, since it was high season. With all of our expensive education, one would have thought that we would have thought of this! By now we were simply exhausted and would have settled for anything. However, as luck would have it, we found a small piece of land that had a camping sign at the entrance. We dragged ourselves in and, much to our amazement, there were no other campers there. We were too tired to even question why; in any case, it only needed to be for one night. We found a rather grungy bathroom, but no owner. Who cares? We set up our four-person framed tent, with some dexterity considering our condition, and just flopped.

Later, I was slowly emerging from one of the deepest sleeps I had ever experienced when I heard music that was extremely loud and confusing, all different tunes being played at the same time. A terrible screeching of tires that could be heard over the shouts and screams of excited people. It seemed that I was experiencing a nightmare that made no sense. But I felt awake! I shook my head a couple of times and still heard the same thing. I focused on Pete who was close by and noticed him laughing at me.

"What the hell is going on," I asked in a dazed manner, still not sure if I was dreaming or not.

"You need to take a look outside. You won't believe what you'll see," he replied.

I dragged myself to the entrance flaps and stuck my head out.

"Oh my God," I shouted above the noise.

This is unbelievable, I thought, somewhat relieved. The whole bedlam was caused by a fair ground located on the other side of the fence from our tent. We were all so tired that we failed to notice it. No wonder there were no other campers in this campground.

One of the more memorable times of our Riccione trip was meeting identical twin German girls. With longish, blondish hair and striking features, they were very beautiful and fun-loving. The only problem was that wherever one went, the other was sure to follow. I guess this was the plan worked out by their "Mutter" and it worked. Nevertheless, we had a wonderful time and by the time the vacation had come to an end, my friendship with Doris had grown quite strong. Even though the twins were truly identical I never had a problem identifying Doris since she spoke English and her sister didn't!

One of the funny things I remember about Doris didn't happen until I returned home. My sister Neenie was anxious to hear all the stories, and when I came to tell her about my new love, I had a hard time saying her name — it was the same as my mother's. For goodness sake, how could I date a girl with the same name as my mother? So when the inevitable question was asked, I changed the pronunciation a little to "Door-es." Well Neenie, just roared with laughter, seeing right through my deception.

"You mean her name is Doris, don't you?" she demanded.

"No, Door-es" I said, emphasising each syllable, as I felt myself blushing. Sisters can be so cruel.

Eventually, I came clean much to Neenie's amusement. It took me a long time to live that one down.

After the holiday ended, Doris and I continued our relationship through frequent letter writing. But after about six months, her letters abruptly stopped. Then, out of the blue, about eight weeks after I had last heard from Doris, I received a letter from Germany from a friend of the family: Doris was dead and her sister was in a coma!

I was alone in London at the time I received the letter and didn't know where to turn. I was truly dazed and upset. Was this some sort of sick joke? Did Doris's family not want me corresponding with Doris and this some extraordinary way for them to tell me? All these ridiculous thoughts went through my mind for a couple of days as I tried to come to terms with the truth. Doris was dead.

Apparently Doris was driving a car with her sister as a passenger when she lost control and the car left the road. It bounced down a slight embankment and stopped abruptly in a ditch. Doris's sister hit her head hard on the windscreen and Doris hit the steering wheel solidly. Seat belts were not automatically installed in those days, and I am sure things would be different if they had been wearing them. Seeing that her sister was badly hurt, Doris climbed out of the car and climbed back to the road to summon help. Apparently, she was conscious all the way to the hospital, obviously concerned about her sister. However, when she reached the hospital she collapsed and never regained consciousness. She died from internal bleeding from a burst spleen.

In true British fashion, tragedies of this type are just brushed away and life goes on as though nothing has happened. I did send a letter of condolences to Doris's family, but never knew whether they received it or even if they cared. Their loss must have been devastating.

Naturally I was upset, but time is a great healer. To help me take my mind of the situation, Pete and I decided it was time for our next holiday. This time we would visit the Costa Brava, on the East Coast of Spain. I had persuaded my mother that I should have a brand new MGB convertible, which was only fair since my brother John had gotten one at the same age.

There was nothing better than travelling through France and Spain in a new blue MGB with the top down. With our hair blowing freely and tanned faces, we turned the heads of many young girls, all the way to our destination. Blanes, I think. Things were looking promising.

The downside to the MGB, if there was one, was that there was very little space for any luggage, so we kept gear to an absolute minimum. This included a two-man tent that Peter said was small, but perfect for the job and a fair amount of food in case the local fare was too local, if you know what I mean. Beverages we felt would be less expensive in Spain, and at least the same quality as we were used to in England.

When we finally arrived in Blanes after what seemed an interminable drive, we were met with torrential rain. The only thing to do was to hit a local bar and relax a little. It was there that we found out that the forecast was not good for the next couple of days. With limited holiday time, we felt that every minute of every day was vital for our mental well-being. This might be overstating it a bit, but we quickly came to the decision that we would continue moving south until the rain stopped, which it did in the resort town of Sitges close to and south of Barcelona.

It didn't take us long to find a campground relatively close to the centre of town. Spain in those days was wonderfully cheap, so we were able to splash out a little on our accommodation. We pitched Pete's two-man tent and unloaded the contents of the overloaded MGB into the tent along with my camp bed and sleeping bag.

"There," I said selfishly, "I'm all set."

Pete, who by this time was looking a little hot and bothered said, "What do you mean."

"Well, we managed to put all the supplies and my bed in the tent, but there is no room for your bed." I said laughingly. "Your error," I declared, "you'll have to find somewhere else to sleep."

"You bugger," he muttered not knowing whether to laugh or cry. Then a strange smile came over his face, as I believe his testosterone was beginning to kick in.

Most nights I was home before him and if he wasn't sleeping somewhere else, he was beneath the tree outside my tent, acting as my guard. Only one night did he get back before me and grabbed my bed. He must have had a sixth sense or else he watched the weather forecast in the bar, since that was the only night that we had rain, and it was a torrential downpour. I spent one of the most uncomfortable nights of my life curled up underneath the tonneau cover in the MGB as it was raining too hard to put the top on, an exercise that took at least 10 minutes. There was no way my six-foot body could comfortably stretch sideways with the gear lever and hand brake in the middle, and I was unable to sit in the seat properly with the tonneau on. Pete got his revenge.

We had many memorable nights in Sitges, but there was one night that will remain with me forever. There was a small nightclub next to the beach, mostly constructed of bamboo and raffia, that had a wonderful South Sea island feel about it. Mostly open to the elements, you could always expect a gentle breeze to blow in from the Mediterranean to cool you on those warm sultry nights of July and August. The crowd at La Cabana, one of the hot spots of Sitges, was always young and energetic.

One night, early in the vacation, I was leaning against a thick bamboo post on the far side of the club sipping a Bacardi and Coke when a group of girls strolled into the club in what appeared to be a nonchalant manner. But we knew their finely tuned scanners were checking out the scene. As they sauntered over to a table on the other side of the dance floor from me, my eyes became fixed on the most striking blonde I had ever seen. She was very tall, about six-feet, with straight, long blonde hair and wearing a very striking black trouser suit with colourful flowers embroidered on it.

I am sure every male and probably most females were looking in the same direction I was. I was mesmerised for a short time, and then I called myself to action. Fortunately, I had already diminished my naturally shy nature with a few Bacardi and Cokes. Without appearing to be overly anxious, I coolly rushed over to the group. The problem, or fun, of situations like this at foreign bars, is that you never know whether the other person speaks English.

The tall blonde was standing with her back to me talking to a group of four or five other girls. My overly polite approach was doomed from the start. I may have been the first there, but I failed to properly catch the blonde's attention.

I said in a courteous and somewhat anxious voice over her shoulder "Would you like to dance?"

"Yes" came the instant reply from the girl I was facing, a brunette.

I was somewhat stunned, but recovered quickly. I danced a couple of dances as I kept an eye on the blonde. She was still standing there, swaying to the music. Were all the guys blind or drunk or maybe they were just blind drunk? Who cares? Their loss was my gain. So without appearing too eager, I suggested to my partner, Willfred, that we go back to the table.

"Hell," I muttered to myself just as we were arriving at the table. There was this tall, heavily tanned and somewhat inebriated good-looking French guy asking the blonde to dance! Gone, I thought to myself, and I was right.

Oh well. My new Dutch acquaintance was good looking, fun-loving, and had an extremely pleasant personality. She also had the advantage of speaking excellent English, which to a person of my linguistic skills was a distinct plus. Seven years of French lessons at school, and I still struggled with the basics of the language. Just as well for Charles' sake, the Frenchman who stole my blonde.

As it turned out the blonde, Suzan, and Willfred were both kindergarten teachers from the Netherlands and were the best of friends, sharing a room at a hotel on the other side of the railway tracks. The only problem I had, if there was one, was to do with the name, again. The only Willfreds I knew were guys, and at 19, this seemed to be an issue with me. Actually, male Willfreds are spelled with one "l" but so what? Her name sounded like a guys' name and this was definitely going to cause embarrassment for a young man like me. Anyway, just like the name Doris, I was sure I would get used to it.

The vacation went all too quickly, and we had many wonderful times together, sometimes with Charles and sometimes without. Days were normally spent on the beach and nights in inexpensive restaurants and nightclubs. But all good things come to an end, especially when it comes to holiday romances. Naturally we were all a little down as our holiday came to a close. Then, out of the blue, with the swapping of addresses and phone numbers well behind us, Suzan asked me whether there was anyone I knew in England who would be interested in having an au pair for a year. This request came as a great shock and a very pleasant surprise. What a break — Suzan wants to live in England for a year! My mind raced as I searched for possible candidates. My eldest sister, who lived near London, had a little girl, and my elder brother and many of his friends had young families — and they all lived very close to me, which was even better.

"Of course," I said without hesitation. "I am sure I can find someone. I will ask around when I get back home," I said assuredly, knowing that this was one task that I was not about to mess up.

Now, I was not aware of the politics that were playing out behind the scenes or if in fact there were any being played out at all, but soon thereafter Willfred approached me with the same request.

"Willfred," I said gently, "I am sure I can find something for you too," which was the truth since everyone was looking out for good au pairs, especially if they came with a reliable reference! Both girls were kindergarten teachers and both spoke English, Willfred better than Suzan.

As we departed Sitges, the scene was set. I was now in the employment agency business, specialising in au pairs. The drive home was uneventful with the exception of driving down the three-mile Mulsanne Straight at the famous Le Mans race track. This part of the track is normally a regular road and tends to bring to the surface the racing blood in anyone who drives it. With both my maternal grandfather Holloway, who raced cars in the early 1900's, and John, who also had a passion for the sport in my family, I felt I definitely had it in my blood. But this was one time when an excess of speed in a motor car didn't turn into an incident.

CHAPTER 9

AU PAIRS

Au pair. Obviously a French phrase, but what does it mean? As I have already alluded to, my French has yet to be perfected, but as far as I can figure it means "something in twos!" This observation proved true when I started my plan to import two Dutch girls to England as au pairs.

I asked around and found out that very good friends of David were expecting their first child. Since Suzan asked me first, it seemed only appropriate that I try to set her up with Neville and Sue. By chance, they lived about four miles from where I was living in Chaddesley Corbett. I have to admit that although I dated Willfred on vacation, I still had a strong infatuation for Suzan. My feelings for Willfred were more of a holiday romance rather than a regular romantic affair.

Soon thereafter, it was announced that my sister, Jayne, and her husband, Nigel, were expecting their second child, so I approached them to see if they would be interested in having a Dutch au pair. Of course, I was thinking that Willfred would fill this position perfectly. Although she would be working near London, she would be working within the family so to speak and therefore I would get to see her on a fairly regular basis. This proposal seemed to be an excellent, if not selfish plan, to me and satisfied the needs of everyone. Boy, was I naïve.

While plans for Suzan to go to Neville and Sue in early January progressed fairly quickly, Willfred was having nothing to do with my plan to place her with Jayne. Understandably, she felt that Suzan had forced herself between us, and she had plans of her own.

Willfred came to England to spend Christmas and New Year's with me, which culminated with a final grand New Year's Eve party at Yesselcote, our family home. The New Year's Eve party at the Bamford's had become well known for its style and merriment, and this the last one before our pending move to Picklewell was no exception. It was held in the garage, adjoining stables, loft, and attached marquee. The ambience was terrific and Donald, a friend of mine, played the discotheque music, which was brand new at that time. The partying really didn't stop until daylight.

Willfred returned to Holland, determined to sort things out for herself. She had managed to find a family in Barnt Green, about 12 miles from Chaddesley, who needed an au pair for their family of three children. I knew nothing of the family, but assumed that Willfred had found them through an agency that would have checked them out. She started in March, and things with the family were fine at first.

Then one very dark wet night the phone rang at Picklewell, my mother's new house. Coincidentally Jayne and Nigel were staying with us. I was out at the time.

On the other end of the line there was a very upset Willfred, who had been thrown out by her au pair family without warning or transportation during a miserable English rain storm. It was incredible how anyone could do this, especially to a young girl from a foreign country. No reason was given, but the general consensus was that the mother of the children was either jealous of Willfred's interaction with the children or a perceived relationship with her husband. Both of these ideas were ridiculous. About half an hour after the call, Nigel picked up a dripping wet and forlorn girl with all her luggage and drove her back to Picklewell. The expression on my face when I nonchalantly walked in for dinner must have been a picture.

It was during Willfred's stay at Picklewell that it was agreed she would go to Jayne and Nigel as their au pair. It seemed that my plan came to pass after all. I still felt it was the right thing to do.

Suzan arrived soon after the birth of Lance. The once great friendship between Willfred and Suzan was now history, and the two were feuding. I had seen this on TV, but in real life this is no joke, and I felt awful about it. But what was I to do? Suzan had felt so bad about the situation that she told Neville that she was no longer going to go out with me.

"That's the most ridiculous thing I've ever heard," Neville said angrily. "If Peter wants to take you out and you want to go out with him, why on earth would you not want to? If he wanted to date Willfred he would. So if he asks you out again you are going." I did and she did.

I didn't date many girls, maybe due to laziness or maybe there was an underlying reason. In any case, I had what I believed was a terrific girlfriend. My sisters felt I should "play the field" a little more, and Neenie particularly was forever trying to fix me up with her friends. She was probably right, but I never felt that anyone I went out with was preferable to Suzan.

After the year came to an end with the Cope family, Suzan told me that it was time for her to return to Holland. Naturally I was devastated. She pointed out that the British immigration law only allowed her to stay for one year but that this could be extended if she found a job and became self-sufficient. In the Netherlands, she was a fully-qualified kindergarten teacher, and we felt that she could easily transfer her qualifications. At that time, England was crying out for qualified teachers but amazingly they wouldn't even look at her qualifications. I even went to the Department of Education in London to plead her case, but it fell on deaf ears.

Suzan then found out that she could become a trainee nurse at the Corbett Hospital about 10 miles away. With a second career in the making, she commenced her State Enrolled Nurse (SEN) course. At 21 years old, she was somewhat older than the other students and her maturity soon put her in a position of responsibility. After only a few months of training she was moved to a geriatric and acute medical unit of the Burton Road Hospital. It is unbelievable to think that she had the responsibility of dispensing drugs and full control of the ward at night time. There wasn't even a doctor on duty. Her routine duties included the constant cleaning of incontinent patients, running after confused patients, and laying out of dead patients. It was not hard to see that the work was taking its toll on her. She was losing weight, looked drawn and, most unlike Suzan, was prone to bouts of crying. But at least she was able to stay in England and took comfort in the fact that this was not a forever job.

CHAPTER 10

PLAYING RUGBY

At Ellesmere, I played rugby football — a sport I was reasonably good at, although not as good as John, and that I enjoyed. I managed to become the first team vice-captain in my last year at school and was thought of as a tough player. This image was important to me as it detracted from any feminine mannerisms I may have exhibited.

After I left Ellesmere, I played for Bromsgrove Town Rugby Football Club. Both David and John were playing there, so of course I was expected to play there too. It was okay to start with, but I always played for the second team and we rarely won. This can soon take the excitement out of the game, and each Saturday it became more of an effort to drag myself off to a game until I finally hung up my boots after three years.

I don't want it to sound as if it was no fun at all — I had some great times at the club. After each game, especially a home game, we would party hard at the clubhouse, with our girlfriends or wives in tow. Beer would flow freely and the infamous rugby songs would become more raucous and obscene as the night went on.

By far the most enjoyable time I had with the rugby club was when we went on tour. My first tour was in the West Country, mostly in the county of Somerset. Somerset is known for its cider apples and the alcoholic cider that is produced there. The rough cider, known as Scrumpy, became the beverage of choice while we were on tour, at least for the first night. This together with a bottle of vodka that someone foolishly produced during the evening made my world spin.

To keep costs down, rooms were shared. John was also touring, so naturally we shared a room. Much to my amazement, our room wasn't equipped with two single beds but one double bed. By the time I rolled into the bedroom I was past caring. John had wisely suggested that I sleep on the side of the bed that was closest to the sink just in case my evening decided to make a sudden reappearance. Considering the state I was, this seemed to be a prudent suggestion.

We went to bed around 2.00 a.m., as we had a game to play the next day. I remember my head being about two feet above the pillow and that was it.

It was still dark outside, and I woke to a terrible noise coming from John's side of the bed as he scrambled over me, flinging himself towards the sink.

"Oh my God," I moaned, as a terrible retching sound erupted next to me.

"Sorry Pete," John groaned, as it became clear to both of us that he hadn't made it. What's more, with all the effort that he had put into his fling across the bed to make it to the sink, he had provoked serious trouble at the other end.

"Oh John, this is disgusting!" I complained bitterly having little regard for his problems. With the awful stench, I was having difficulty keeping things to myself as well.

"Sorry Pete," John reiterated.

John swore several times and said he would clean it up. For me, the night was over. I moved out of the bedroom to a chair on the landing and tried to sleep, with no success. Sometime later John poked his head out of the door to announce that the room was "as clean as a whistle."

"Some whistle," I murmured as I did an about turn to return to my chair.

With no hangover and a good night's rest, John played some excellent rugby the next day. Fortunately for me, I was not scheduled to play in that match. The tour continued as planned and was followed up the next year with another one in Dublin, Ireland. So with two rugby tours under my belt, my masculinity was firmly established.

PART 3
EARLY ADULTHOOD

CHAPTER 11

FAMILY FIRST

In the '60s and '70s, couples were getting married in their early 20s. I was in no mood to buck the trend; in fact, it was important for me to go with societal standards to avoid my transsexualism being detected — my biggest fear. With a holiday house in Seaview now at my disposal, I was able to experiment with my female side less privately as I felt comfortable enough there to walk in the village at night. But the fear of being caught and exposed was ever present.

Sex change operations from male to female were becoming more prevalent. With Dr. Burou in Casablanca willing and able to perform vaginoplasty, many girls went there to fulfill their dreams. Some girls made the headlines like April Ashley and Jan Morris (both British), while most were quietly absorbed into society as females. In the back of my mind, I also felt that I someday would be one of these quiet females, but how and when, only God knew. However, the operation wasn't yet mainstream and wasn't allowed in most medically advanced countries.

In the meantime, although there was no defining moment, I decided that when I married it would not be to an English girl for fear that I would bring harm and disgrace to that family. As illogical and crazy as this sounds now, that is how I thought and felt at the time — no one ever said that teenagers make sense.

My love for Suzan had become very strong over the previous four years, so I broached the subject of marriage with her. She was thrilled at the prospect, and we decided to get engaged in the Netherlands after I had asked her father's permission.

After a truly wonderful wedding in Chaddesley Church, a reception in a marquee at Picklewell, and a honeymoon in Verbier, Switzerland, Suzan and I set about the awkward situation of two people trying to live together for the first time. For anyone who has been through it, you will know what I mean: if you can get through the first year, then the worst is behind you. Fortunately, true love helps enormously, but even with a strong, loving relationship, squabbles and arguments will inevitably happen.

Our first year was little different from others, except that I was probably more emotional than most husbands. There were times I would be sitting on the floor, completely unable to control my anxiety. I couldn't figure out what was wrong with me, and poor Suzan was at her wits end. She later confided in me that after three months of marriage, she started to wonder if she had made the right decision. It wasn't that we didn't love each other — I was pretty unpredictable and hard to live with.

She didn't know what the problem was, nor did I. I knew it didn't have to do with Suzan or our marriage, although Suzan took the brunt of my outbursts. I knew I hated my work at Touche Ross and had the pressure of trying to pass my final exams, both of which might have had a bearing on the problem. Nonetheless, I would crash down to a low, and then we would go for weeks with some pretty good times. I am sure, subconsciously, that my transsexual feelings were playing a role, although I was suppressing those as hard as I could. Normally, the smallest, insignificant thing would set me off. However, despite all the ups and downs we still managed to enjoy our marriage and our love for each other grew stronger because of the problems we overcame.

For all of her life, Suzan lived in a small apartment on the Noordendÿk in Dordrecht. Her parents were married soon after World War II had ended. The Dutch government set about rebuilding Holland, which had been badly damaged, first by the German invasion and then by the Allied Forces liberating the Dutch. The apartment building into which Suzan's parents moved was the first of many in the development on this site, and Suzan's parents were the first family to move in. That earned them some publicity and the right to receive the key for their apartment from the mayor of Dordrecht.

Living in a third floor apartment, Suzan, as a child, was never allowed to have a pet any bigger than a guinea pig. After we were married and lived at Badge Court Cottage in the beautiful English countryside, she decided it was time for her to have the dog she had always longed for. I have to admit that I really wasn't paying much attention to the chatter about her getting a dog, as I had always had a dog while growing up so it seemed quite natural to me. I should have paid more attention. I was right about the dog being no big thing; it was a HUGE thing. A bloodhound. A pedigree bloodhound. An expensive pedigree bloodhound. As a puppy, Caesar was the most adorable dog: black and tan with more skin than he would ever need, even as a big dog! He was so big as a puppy that we were not allowed to walk him for several months until his bones had a chance to grow. Once he was allowed to go on walks, Suzan walked him every day, rain, sleet, snow, or shine. He was definitely her dog, and she took extraordinary care of him. She took him to dog shows several times, once at the major show in England, Crufts. He placed several times, but never first.

Within the year we had a second bloodhound. This one came from a family who owned a pub and were unable to cope with him. Why we took him only Suzan knows. His pedigree was not as good as Caesar's, as if I cared, but Basil's demeanour was much better. The two of them were quite a handful to care for, especially the constant drooling and slobbering. Having said all that, I was very fond of them, and they were very loyal to Suzan and me.

When we first got Caesar, he slept under the counter in our kitchen. This was not the most idyllic or hygienic situation, so when Basil arrived, Suzan asked me if I could build a kennel for them. The design requests were quite specific. The floor had to be at least 6 inches off the ground. It must have a window and some sort of venting system to allow the air to circulate and some sort of heating system to keep the chill off them in the winter.

I set about this project with vigour and much to Suzan's and my delight, it turned out very well. I think the dogs also appreciated it, although they never seemed that happy about being put in there for the night. As it turned out this was the first of numerous DIY projects I eventually carried out and continue to undertake even to this day.

Suzan decided that we were not going to start a family until we had been married at least one year. I don't know where these ideas are formulated, but I was not about to argue with her reasoning. It wasn't long after our first wedding anniversary that Suzan came home from a doctor's appointment with the news that she was pregnant.

"Well that's wonderful news," I said feeling a little stunned. I didn't know if I was up to the responsibility of having a child to look after, but I knew that Suzan was more than ready. I told my mother, who was very excited about her fifth grandchild. But Suzan's parents were, understandably, the most excited at the thought of becoming Oma and Opa for the first time. You could almost hear the sound of the knitting needles clattering across the North Sea.

Suzan had a wonderful first pregnancy. Everything was normal. The doctor started to ask Suzan at which hospital she planned to have her baby once her due date started approaching.

"Could I have mine at home?" Suzan shyly asked the doctor, expecting an instant rejection since this practice was quickly dying out in England.

"What a good idea, my dear. Don't go to one of those sausage factories," came back the doctor's surprising reply.

Home deliveries, with the help of a midwife and doctor, still occurred but much less frequently than in the past. The medical profession obviously prefers to have all the equipment a hospital provides in case something should go wrong.

Arrangements were made for our first child to be born at Badge Court Cottage. As soon as Suzan's water broke, we were told to call for the midwife. She would take care of the whole procedure, up to the point of birth when the doctor would be called for. Simple procedures to follow, which we did on the evening of December 3, 1971. My mother came over to keep me, and my bottle of Scotch, company downstairs while the midwife accompanied Suzan upstairs. Several hours passed with little to no action. Then, at about 2:00 p.m. the midwife told us that things were coming to a head. She asked me if I wanted to attend the birth, which took me completely by surprise. I had never even considered it, but thought it would be a wonderful thing to witness the birth of my first child. So I eagerly agreed but then realised that my mother was being left out. Fortunately, she had the good sense to ask whether she could watch as well — although she had birthed five children of her own, she had never witnessed a birth. The midwife asked Suzan, who, by now, couldn't have cared less if the whole world was watching. The scene was set.

Much to my amazement, the midwife wanted me to play an active role. I thought I was just going to sit back and watch the event, but this was not how it would be. My job was to kneel on the bed and push Suzan's left leg and knee back towards her head. I had absolutely no I idea what I was doing or why I was doing it, but it seemed to work! Slowly but surely, a small head began to appear. It truly was the most amazing sight I have ever witnessed. Sections of the child's skull appeared to me to be overlapping each other so as to make the head smaller. As soon as the whole head was out then immediately all the pieces went back together again, as they should. After the head was out, the rest of the body came out with a rush. There were a few small cries, and Deborah Suzanna was alive and well in this world. A truly natural birth. The doctor arrived about 15 minutes after Debbie was born to check out mother and child. After administering a few sutures, he was on his way.

From my perspective, the whole procedure from beginning to end couldn't have been easier, but it all seemed so unreal. There we were, a few hours earlier, just the two of us sitting down to dinner as we had done since we had been married, and now there were three of us. Debbie lay in her crib staring at the bright light and hiccuping. She hadn't even had anything to eat or drink yet. She cried a little when she was born, and hardly ever cried again. My little daughter, 21 inches long and weighing seven and a half pounds. A truly amazing event.

I have to admit I was a very proud father and enjoyed all the attention my little family was getting. Even though babies are born every second around the world, it somehow seems so very important and different when it is your child. I guess I didn't really understand how having a baby in our family was going to affect our lifestyle. On the one hand, we wanted to be very responsible parents and on the other, we (mainly I) were loath to give up our previous lifestyle of going to dinner parties with our friends, visiting pubs in the evenings, sailing on the south coast, or following John and his car racing team. Somehow in the beginning we still did it all. Debbie was small enough that she could come with us in her carry crib to the dinner parties or travel in the car with us everywhere, and we still felt we were being responsible. But I knew down the road that something had to give.

CHAPTER 12

FREEZING PIPES

B adge Court Cottage was an appealing little old black and white cottage with three bedrooms upstairs and a bathroom off the dining room downstairs. The small living room was the cosiest room in the house, having large heavy beams and a massive fireplace with a copper canopy. The cottage had been enlarged, so our bedroom and the kitchen were a good size. The garden was small, but secure and the western views over miles of English countryside were simply beautiful. It was located opposite a working blacksmith's shop, although most of the smithy's work was done at the stables rather than at the shop. The cottage was a wedding gift from my mother to us. She bought it from good friends of mine, who had also used it as their starter home.

What a wonderful home in which to begin married life. Small, inexpensive to run, and full of charm. It was actually a semi-detached house, the other half owned by a local family who thought that their adult son might live there eventually. It had been uninhabited for many years previously and remained so for the entire time we lived there. Previous owners of Badge Court Cottage and I had ideas of converting the two cottages into one house, which would have worked perfectly since it would have made a nice size house, and the garden of the other cottage was quite a bit larger. But the owner was steadfast; he was not going to sell.

We lived in that little cottage for two and a half years. A perfect place to bring up Debbie, but not so perfect for two large bloodhounds. The cottage needed very little renovation before we moved in. The only improvement we made was a pedestal basin in our bedroom since the bathroom downstairs was quite a hike, even though the cottage was small.

The way plumbers install their pipes in England leads one to believe that the weather was akin to that of the Mediterranean. For although it invariable freezes many times in the winter, the drain pipes and sometimes the water supply pipes are installed on the outside of older homes, as was the case at Badge Court Cottage.

One night, Suzan woke up to the sound of dripping water. The pedestal sink was on her side of the bed. She got out of bed to turn the tap off, only to find that the sink was full of water and overflowing. She let out a howl in her Dutch accent, "Pee-teer," which caught my attention even from a deep sleep.

"The sink is over flowing" she continued.

"Oh hell" I muttered as I stumbled out of bed in the nude, which was my normal nightly dress code.

As I came around to her side of the bed to carry out an inspection, it was now my turn to shriek.

"Oh shit, what the hell was that — aagh, that hurts," I cried out loud.

"What is it?" Suzan said in a matter of fact manner, as only Suzan can. "I'll put the lights on" she continued, which struck me as an excellent idea.

"God damn it Suzan" I said angrily as I found the cause of my pain to be the three prong plug of her Carmen rollers, which were lying on the floor, digging into the sole of my foot. You would have thought that with all this commotion, pain, and suffering I would have been wide-awake. Not so.

I checked out the sink and sure enough it was overflowing. The freezing weather outside had caused the drain to block and a dripping tap had filled the sink to overflowing. Just as I was thinking where all this water was going I heard another shriek from Suzan, who was now downstairs.

"Pee-teer, come here quickly!"

There was that certain tone in her voice that made me think it was urgent. It was freezing outside and not much warmer inside. Time to put on some clothing I decided. I grabbed a sweater and slid into my jeans.

"Shit — aagh — fuck," I screamed again.

"What is it"? Suzan shouted back with somewhat more concern.

I was in too much pain and agony to answer back. In any case, it was taking all my concentration trying to untangle the skin of my private parts from my zipper.

When I finally arrived downstairs, I found a very dangerous scene. Directly beneath the sink was a small cloakroom with a small, but pretty chandelier. It was a beautiful sight really. The light had been switched on by Suzan, and the glass and cascading water were twinkling in its light. I turned the light off as Suzan continued to mop the wooden floor.

Since the dripping tap could not be stopped, I had to unplug the drain. Suzan boiled a kettle of water, and with the help of a short ladder and the light from the porch, I went outside and started to pour boiling water on the pipe above my head. A very bad idea.

I was getting tired of all this pain. I screamed and swore out loud again, as the boiling water ran down my arm scalding me.

"Ssshh Peter," Suzan whispered loudly, "the neighbours." I was too tired and upset to reply, even though I knew what I wanted to say. After five minutes of using hot water — as opposed to boiling water — the drain cleared.

"I'm going to bed" I declared, not even caring whether the drain froze up again.

I dried myself, crawled upstairs, and climbed between the cold sheets, totally exhausted. I awoke the next morning wondering if I had had a terrible nightmare but all my scrapes, sores, and scalds made me realise that I had really endured it all.

The first years of marriage were somewhat strange to me. We socialised at many dinner parties, had fun in the Isle of Wight, enjoyed skiing in the Alps, played on the many boats, and just cherished Debbie's company. This joy was mixed with lows and heavy drinking. I often used to take long walks down the country lanes to try and sort things out in my mind but nothing came of it.

CHAPTER 13

SAILING ADVENTURES

Rozango. Such a perfect name for a beautiful sailing boat. I am not sure who came up with it; I think it might have been Rosie Burton, the wife of John Burton. Both are good friends of ours, although at the time they were probably better friends of my brother John, as they were good car racing pals. But soon after they were married, I think Rosie managed to persuade John that motor racing was a little dangerous, especially while raising a family, and that he should find another sport to enjoy.

He chose sailing and bought every book and magazine about sailing to learn as much as possible about the sport. I am not sure why, but he approached me to see if I was interested in buying a sailing boat with him. Well that was music to my ears since sailing was in my blood and I had given up on the sport of powerboat racing because it was too expensive. It seemed that the boat owner with most money always won — hardly fair.

John had done his research before approaching me and said that he had found a French-built 33-foot boat that showed promise. He showed me the particulars, and it was definitely the right price for a 6-berth, aft cabin sailing sloop. He had arranged for a trial sail down in Southampton on the south coast of England and suggested that I joined him. I jumped at the chance.

The following Saturday I found myself aboard a reasonably well-built, 33-foot sloop called Fandango with a nicely fitted out interior. There were just three of us, the salesman, John and me. As we prepared to take the boat out for a sail, the salesman, who for obvious reasons had taken the helm of the boat, asked John and me to set the sails. Well the genoa was still in the sail bag, so I took that up to the bow, and John followed me.

"How do we set the sails?" John asked nervously. "Do you know how to put this thing up?" he said pointing to the mass of sails on the fore deck.

I was somewhat shocked as I thought that John had some knowledge of sailing, but I began to realise he had never been on a sailing boat before. Anything he knew about sailing boats he had garnered from the books.

Fortunately, I was able to literally show him the ropes, and I don't think our salesman was any the wiser. Even though I obviously knew much more about sailing than John, I was happy to be persuaded by John that this boat would suit our needs well. It was soon after that we became proud, joint owners of Rosango. The name was an anagram of Rosie, Suzan, and Fandango.

Sharing one's toys is never easy but in this case it wasn't too bad. The biggest problem was that John and I approached our sailing from different perspectives. I was interested in just cruising around and visiting all the little ports in the Solent, staying the night, visiting the pubs and restaurants, and generally having a good time. John couldn't go anywhere in Rosango without racing some other boat on the water, whether they knew it or not. He was forever trying to garner every ounce of speed out of the boat. I must say that for a complete novice he learned quickly how to sail competently. I was never concerned about him taking the boat out, although I don't think he felt the same about me. He was always concerned that I would stretch the sails, as I would only reef down when absolutely necessary, preferring to have the water on my gunwales. It wasn't long after we had had the boat that John suggested we add a folding propeller so that the boat would move faster. Then it was rod rigging instead of the customary wire rigging to make the mast stiffer. Then there was an extra sail of this type or that. There were little tweaks here and bigger tweaks there which were all coming out of our joint bank account! All of these ideas, I'm sure, were coming out of the sailing magazines that he incessantly read.

I never regretted purchasing Rozango and had many wonderful weekends on her. Mike & Rosie often joined us, as did other friends. Since the boat slept six in three separate cabins, we were all very comfortable. Rosie always said that I had a total change in personality when aboard Rosango. I apparently became (slightly) tyrannical the moment I stepped on board. Even though she said she quite liked it, I strongly denied it. However, I was the captain and had the awesome responsibility of keeping the boat and its crew safe. Given the crew, this was almost an impossible task!

On one occasion we had anchored a couple of miles up the Medina River from Cowes. There was a paddle steamer moored there at the time, which served as a restaurant and nightclub — an excellent place to stop for a night. The next day we set off for a different port but found it difficult to sail on the narrow river, so we motored down and docked at Cowes to pick up some supplies. Suzan had decided to stay on board as the rest of us went into town. For some reason, presumably to impress me, Suzan decided to prepare the genoa ready for hoisting. I had impressed upon my crew that it was very important that we look professional and that the sails were hoisted quickly and proficiently. Now Suzan felt nervous and asked me if I would check her handy work, so Mike and I went to the foredeck and checked that no lines were twisted and that the cleats were on the forestay in order. After all it was close to Cowes week, the premier sailing event in England, and we were passing right in front of the Royal Yacht Squadron, the most prestigious yacht club in England, if not the world.

My crew was the usual: Mike, Rosie, and Suzan. We entered the harbour from our dock and continued to motor through all the fabulous yachts moored there and passed the quay on the water front, which was lined with crowds of onlookers. As we approached the Royal Yacht Squadron at the junction of the Medina River and the Solent, I shouted the command to hoist the foresail. Mike immediately and enthusiastically sprang into action, pulling on the genoa halyard as both he and I watched it go up. The only difference between us was that Mike seemed genuinely pleased with his effort and I was astounded.

"Get that fucking sail down," I screamed with all my might. Mike swung around and looked at me in bewilderment.

"Get it down, get it down," I screamed again at Mike. With his customary cigarette still in his mouth, he sprung onto the fore deck and started to pull the sail down. By this time my conniption fit had focused Rosie and Suzan's attention on the foresail and me.

"What's the matter," everyone demanded at once.

"If you hadn't noticed," I said, "the damn sail was upside down with the sail head at the bottom."

Mike was a little embarrassed, but Rosie and Suzan were annoyingly amused. Needless to say the captain was not amused.

We owned the boat for two seasons before John and I decided it was time to sell the boat. For me, with my new family obligations, this was one of the things that had to go. The boat was impractical for our family and too far away. I don't think Suzan ever really enjoyed it, but for Debbie, who was only on the boat a few times, I believe it was the start of her love of sailing, which matured later in her life. John had designs on an ocean racing boat, and I couldn't partner him on that expensive venture. He took the sport seriously and raced as much as he could, although getting a competent crew together was always a problem.

CHAPTER 14

UPPER BIRCH

I t was becoming obvious to both Suzan and I that Badge Court Cottage was too small, especially with two bloodhounds, and it was a very long drive for me to Bridgnorth where I was working at my accounting firm of Thompson and Bamford. I was always on the lookout for houses for sale, especially on the Bridgnorth side of Kidderminster. One day I saw a "For Sale" sign and decided to take a look. I couldn't believe my eyes. It looked like a large house, but not too large, on some beautifully kept grounds. This was definitely worth further inspection. I rushed home and told Suzan about it and said that she had to see it immediately. Suzan stopped making dinner, we dropped Debbie off with our neighbour, and went back to the house. We drove down the red tarmac driveway where our eyes feasted on large beautifully kept lawns, a huge 350-year-old oak tree, and peacocks strutting around the grounds!

Although the "For Sale" sign said "By appointment only" we decided to knock on the door. We asked the owner whether we could see the house, and I think our enthusiasm and youthfulness must have intrigued them because they let us in. They told us that they had decided to move to Sussex and were selling the house and farm separately. It was a very fine house with large rooms, lots of oak panelling, a lovely inglenook fireplace in the living room, a fully fitted library, and a wonderful dining hall. The only

room that needed attention was the kitchen, which meant we could reno-
vate it the way we wanted.

The house was situated on five acres: one and a half acres of field; one acre
of kitchen gardens with three large, if not dilapidated, greenhouses; one
acre of orchards; and one and a half acres of gardens. Suzan and I were so
excited it was hard for us to control our emotions. They told us they had an
offer, but it was by two men, and they would much rather see the house go
to a young couple with a family. We had been seriously thinking of invest-
ing in an apartment in Verbier but realised that this house would be an
investment in our future home. Real estate prices had been rising in England, so we felt we could sell Badge Court Cottage easily and for a good
price. After some hard haggling with several counter offers, we acquired the
house. Fortunately we were able to sell badge Court Cottage for three times
more than had been paid for it two years earlier.

Our move was very easy since the cottage was so small, and we hadn't lived
there long enough to collect too much junk. The most amazing thing was
that when we placed our furniture in Upper Birch, other than the dining
hall, it seemed fully furnished. This was partly due to the warm look of the
panelling — and that we had somehow crammed an awful lot of furniture
into the cottage. Suzan used some of her money to purchase some very fine
antique oak dining room furniture, which suited the house perfectly.

We loved living there. We both enjoyed working in the garden, I in the
kitchen garden and Suzan in the main garden. I bought a small tractor to
mow the lawns, which took me the best part of a day. And of course, the
dogs loved the extra room they had to run and play.

We hadn't been in Upper Birch more than a week when we both had the
scare of our lives. Debbie, who was now five months old, wasn't feeling
well, and Suzan had taken her to the doctor. She was running a temperature
and had bad diarrhea. The doctor diagnosed her as having gastro-enteritis
and gave her some medicine to take. We were not unduly concerned, but

kept an eye on her. The next day, a Saturday, Mike and Rosie were coming over for the evening to help christen our new home. There was a knock at the door, and there were Mike and Rosie with a bottle of champagne. At the same time, there was a cry from upstairs — Suzan. I rushed up to see Suzan hovering over Debbie, who had started to convulse. Her little legs were banging on the floor uncontrollably and Suzan had placed a pillow there to prevent her from hurting herself. The Faulkes' had also come up stairs to see what all the commotion was about. It couldn't have been a worse time for them to arrive; on the other hand they were there to give us moral support. Suzan instructed me to call the doctor and ask him to come quickly, as it was an emergency and asked Rosie to get some cold water so she could swab Debbie down to help get her temperature down. Mike was a little concerned about the temperature of the champagne.

The doctor arrived within 10 minutes, which considering where we lived was remarkably quick. He spent about two minutes with Debbie, gave her an injection, and said that she needed to go to the hospital immediately. I was somewhat panicked and told him that I didn't know where the new Kidderminster hospital was located.

"Follow me," he said.

I knew the situation was particularly serious when I saw how fast the doctor was driving. It was hard to keep up with him. With Debbie on Suzan's lap — no car seats in those days — we eventually arrived at the paediatric department of the hospital. Debbie was rushed off with an Indian doctor while we checked her in. A nurse kindly came over to us to tell us that Dr. Singh was going to take care of her. In a very prejudiced and panicked moment I made a comment that I have regretted for the rest of my life.

"Are you sure he knows what he is doing?" I said to a stunned nurse.

"Dr. Singh is the leading physician of the paediatric department," she replied curtly as she swung around and stormed off.

I guess that all of us have said something, written something, or done something that we have truly regretted at some point in our lives. This was one of those occasions.

Poor Debbie had to have a lumbar puncture to see if she had meningitis. Fortunately, it was gastro-enteritis, and her convulsing fit was from the high temperature.

We returned home where we had left Mike and Rosie looking after the dogs. Rosie said that she last saw Mike flying past the window with the dogs on their leash and his heels dug into the lawn, tearing up the grass. The thought of this and the champagne made us all feel a lot better. Debbie made a full recovery after five days in hospital.

The five acres of grounds kept us busy, especially the gardens. The one and a half acres of field weren't being utilised, so our old neighbour, the black-smith's wife, Wendy, wanted to know if she could use the field to graze her horse, Kagaloop. As you may remember, I am not a horse person, and neither is Suzan. We were intimidated by the size and strength of this ani-mal. This one-time racehorse needed company, so Wendy borrowed a pony, which worked well at first. Both the pony and the horse felt it necessary to chew the bark of our fruit trees in the orchard, so we decided to move them to our field. That meant they had to walk through a small section of our garden. The plan was for me to lead the pony with the aid of a halter, and Kagaloop would automatically follow. I told Suzan to stand at a point in the garden and wave her arms up and down if Kagaloop tried to walk in the wrong direction. The plan did not work well. Kagaloop, seeing the large expanse of green lawns and well-kept gardens, decided to go in that direc-tion. Suzan stood there motionless in fear. The horse was free and trotted over my beautifully manicured lawn, placing huge hoof prints all over the place while I was stuck with a pony. I knew there was a reason why I didn't like horses.

Wendy decided that she would give us a white nanny goat instead of the pony to keep Kagaloop happy. Unfortunately, the goat was more interested in our kitchen garden than keeping a horse company. Every time the goat escaped, which it did just by climbing the gate, it would head straight for our vegetables. One day Suzan had had enough and decided that the goat must go back to Wendy. She thought that Wendy had transported the goat in her estate car,[4] so Suzan decided she would do the same. She tied the rope holding the goat to the dog cage in the car and then went around to the back and just pushed and pushed until the nanny goat went in. She carefully drove the 10 miles to Wendy's house. When she arrived she found Lionel, the blacksmith, and told him she had brought the nanny goat back.

"Oh do you have a trailer?" Lionel asked surprised.

"No," Suzan replied, "I put him in the back of my estate car. Wendy had said that she transported the goat in her estate car."

"In the back of your estate car!" Lionel uttered in complete amazement. As Lionel and his assistant walked outside to witness this sight, he explained to Suzan that Wendy had only used a trailer to transport the goat, never her car.

They arrived at the car, and the two men stared in complete disbelief. Suzan had parked the car on a small bank off the road. The goat was snugly fitted in the back, the windows were all steamed up and a healthy dose of urine was pouring from under the door! Fortunately, the back of the estate car was all rubber and easily cleaned.

We had many visitors, especially from Holland. Suzan's parents were the first to come over, and they were overcome by the size of the house. Although it didn't seem that big to us, the house was ridiculously large to them, especially to Suzan's father. It wasn't hard to understand their feel-

---

4. A station wagon

ings, especially when you consider that their apartment was about the same size as our living room.

Much to my delight, Suzan and Willfred soon patched up their differences, which is what you would expect of true friends. And that is what Willfred was to us, a truly good friend. When she was having problems with her American boyfriend in Holland she came to stay with us to get away from him. She was also looking for a job somewhere in England or continental Europe. As it turned out she stayed several months and eventually landed an excellent job in Zurich, Switzerland.

CHAPTER 15

JEREMY

After giving birth to Debbie, Suzan had trouble getting pregnant again. Apparently she had a tilted womb, which, according to the doctors, was the problem. In my opinion, I would have thought it didn't matter which way the womb faces since one can be at all angles, if you know what I mean. I suppose the doctors knew what they were talking about since they gave Suzan some terrible contraption to be placed inside her and apparently it worked. The dates were calculated and the baby was due on October 31, 1974, Halloween night.

Suzan immediately called her mother to tell her the good news. No one loves children more than Oma, and now she was to get her second grandchild.

"It's going to be a boy on my birthday", Oma stated, her birthday being November 1. We were not about to disagree with her wisdom, but I thought it was a bit of a tall order.

Again, Suzan requested and was granted an at home birth. Midnight passed and November 1 had arrived. By two a.m., the action had started to heat up. Suzan was struggling a bit and things were not as easy as they had been for Debbie's birth. I felt that this was partly due to the fact that I was not carrying out my job on Suzan's left leg, as I did with Debbie's birth.

Suzan's threshold for pain is considerably higher than most of us — she doesn't even have her mouth numbed when she has a filling done at the dentist! The midwife began to administer her a gas to dull the pain, and Suzan began to ask for more, an unusual oddity. The pain must have been severe. Then a crisis occurred: The gas ran out, and neither the doctor nor nurse had an extra bottle. The doctor ordered me to go to the hospital and pick up some more. In many ways, I was somewhat relieved to be able to get some fresh air. Much to my surprise, when he said get a bottle he meant for me to go to the storeroom and pick up a bottle. I thought I just had to ask someone.

"You know where the hospital is, don't you?" the doctor quizzed me.

"Yes," I replied having done the trip several times when Debbie was there.

The doctor then started giving me specific instructions for how to get to the bottle storeroom. He gave me a key and gave exact details as to how the bottle looked, size, and colour codes. He impressed on me how important it was for me to get the right bottle. It seemed so surreal at the time.

Off I went, driving as fast as I dared, with a good excuse up my sleeve should the police stop me. I did exactly as I was told and found the storeroom that was filled with all types of colour-coded bottles. I quickly found mine then hurried back home. I rushed upstairs only to find that the baby's head was nearly out. My mind was racing. How is Suzan? Did she have much pain without the gas? How's the baby? Everyone was so focused that no one noticed that I was back.

All of a sudden the baby was out. The doctor and nurse seemed to be working frantically, and I was not sure why. The baby looked very blue and wasn't crying. After what seemed to be an eternity, the doctor gave the baby a hard smack and out came a howl. The tension that filled the room immediately eased, and the doctor announced that it was a baby boy!

"How about that," I said to Suzan as I gave her a kiss. She smiled, as she lay there totally exhausted, not even able to talk. The midwife did all the things that midwives do and presented him to Suzan. She just gave Jeremy a quick glance over, I suppose to make sure that he was alright, and then told the him that she would see him tomorrow! The doctor explained to me that the baby had a very large head, which gave Suzan a rough time. Also he was born with the umbilical cord wrapped around his neck, which was why he was blue. As the saying goes, all is well that ends well, which in this story it certainly did, especially since Oma's prophecy came true. By midday Oma was sitting on Suzan's bed, cradling Jeremy with a tear in her eye. "This is the best birthday present I have ever had," she announced. The other happy ending to this story is that Willfred accepted our request for her to be Jeremy's godmother.

CHAPTER 16

FACING FEARS

We often went on holiday with Mike and Rosie, but never skiing — they both preferred to bake in the sun, true sun worshippers. Over the years we went to Spain, France, Malta, and Majorca. John and Mary, Rosie's brother and sister-in-law, lived at that time in Nassau, Bahamas. Mike and Rosie had visited them before, but this time we were invited along. As with any holiday, visiting friends who know the area is a great benefit. This was no exception. John took us to an uninhabited island for the day. It was so peaceful having this huge beach to ourselves, which Rosie immediately took advantage by going topless.

The beautifully clear, turquoise water and the fine, white sand made an indelible impression in my mind — as did my stepping on a sea urchin when I was preparing to water ski behind John's boat. Of course we went to other little known beaches where we just relaxed and sustained ourselves with food and drink.

Mike had mentioned that the last time they visited they went island hopping, visiting small villages on other islands. There was regular air service to most of the inhabited islands, so we decided to visit Eleuthera, one of the Windward Islands in the eastern Caribbean. To get the most out of the day we had an early start, early for a holiday that is. We checked in at the airport at Nassau and had a little time to wait for our flight. We passed the time by watching small passenger planes take off and land. Mike and I were somewhat amused by an Empire Airline DC3. The DC3 is an old twin-engine plane that sits on a small rear wheel so that its fuselage is at an angle when the plane is stationary. Interestingly enough this aircraft was the workhorse of the Berlin airlift in the '50s. Neither of us had ever heard of Empire Airlines, and we wondered who would book flights with them if that were the type of plane they were operating.

I don't know why, but I had a fear of flying. Maybe it's purely because it is so unnatural for man to fly. Also, the possibility of a plane crash. It's so devastating, so final. In a car crash, of which I have had many, you don't necessarily die; in fact I don't think I ever had so much as a scratch. Just like myself, Mike wasn't comfortable flying either. We were white-knuckled flyers who would light up a cigarette immediately after the no smoking sign went out to steady our nerves. Mike had assured me that the island planes were modern and safe. As we waited for our flight to be called an announcement was made that the flight to Eleuthera had been cancelled due to mechanical problems — not a good sign. However, they were trying to find another plane and would update us on the situation shortly.

The good news soon came, as they had procured another aircraft and that we would be boarding promptly. There were only about 10 of us on the flight, and we were ushered out of the terminal to our waiting aircraft with little to no formalities. Mike and I felt fortunate that we were getting a close view of the DC3 as we passed it by on the way to our plane. As we walked closer, a smiling, smartly dressed stewardess poked her head out of the fuselage door. Our usher was now directing us straight towards the plane, the DC3. The amusing and caustic comments by Mike and I stopped abruptly.

"They have got to be joking!" Mike and I said simultaneously.

The girls were laughing at us but I think it was also a nervous laugh. We literally climbed into the plane and walked uphill to our seats, grabbing the side handles to pull ourselves forward. We plonked ourselves down into our well-worn seats; I decided to sit next to the window. The air-hostess came around asking our names, presumably to check against the passenger list to make sure we were all legitimate passengers. Mike said it was so that they could notify our next of kin.

Our pilot walked up the aisle, looking more like a bush pilot than an airline pilot. He left the door of the cockpit open as he started the engines. There was a deafening sound of a piston engine and white smoke poured out of one, then the other. By this time both Mike and I had white knuckles, and the plane hadn't even moved. As the pilot revved up the engines, the smoke subsided a bit, but they didn't sound like they were running on all cylinders. Nevertheless, the pilot decided to move to the entrance of the runway where he kept revving up the engines as we bounced around the shaking plane.

Eventually the pilot seemed happy, as he moved the plane forward onto the runway and gave it full throttle. While we gathered speed, the tail began to lift, which made me, and I am sure everyone else, more comfortable. For some reason, the pilot decided to leave the cockpit door open for the flight. We could all peer down the aisle and see the inner sanctum. We felt the plane leave the ground, which was a huge relief since Mike and I had our doubts as to whether this machine could even fly. We were about 30 seconds into our flight when a loud bell went off in the cockpit. Everyone tensed up and focused their eyes in that direction when another bell started. From my seat on the side, I could also see a red light. Even though the bells stopped, my heart was pounding in my chest. I didn't know what to think. The plane kept climbing when it started to make a turn to the left. Mike turned to me with an ashen face and declared that the pilot should have turned to the right if he was going to Eleuthera. The pilot announced that he was returning to the airport as we began to circle. I turned around to say something to the flight attendant, sitting behind me, but decided not to since she looked petrified.

After what seemed like an hour — it really had been minutes — the pilot made a full circle and was approaching land. I never felt that he was in complete control of the aircraft as it bounced around, the engines still not sounding right. As the plane went lower and lower, my knuckles went whiter and whiter. Then suddenly the runway appeared beneath us, and the wheels quickly touched the ground. The plane slowed, and we all dropped back into a sloping position as the rear wheel touched the ground. Mike and I were drained as we crawled out of the plane. We were ushered back into the terminal where we immediately spotted a bar. Even though it was only 9:30 a.m., we ordered two large Bacardi and Cokes — definitely what the doctored ordered after a truly hair-raising experience.

The day was not lost though. The airline found us another aircraft, this time one of their regular, modern planes. We experienced a very interesting day on Eleuthera. The village we visited was all decked out with flags and bunting. This must have been a fête day for them, although we hardly saw a soul.

After many years of flying, most of my fears have disappeared. Initially, much of this had to do with Peter Laing, who had learned to fly while at Liverpool University. Not only did he learn to fly the right way up, but also upside down. Apparently he took great delight in performing stunts over Blackpool Beach, scaring the crowds half to death.

Pete enjoyed flying so much that he decided to make a career of it. He trained with British European Airways (BEA) and became a qualified pilot. The mere thought of Pete being responsible for flying passengers around Europe made me shudder. I knew how Pete thought, and it wasn't always responsibly. I must admit however, BEA had more sense than I gave them credit for. His first long-term assignment was flying cargo planes. Maybe I am being a little harsh, as Pete went on to be a Captain with British Airways and flew the latest Boeing 747 jumbo jets around the world.

One day I happened to mention to Pete my fear of flying.

"Oh, I can get you over that," he said confidently "just come and fly with me in a small plane, and I will show you how everything works. That will help you overcome your fear."

"I'm not so sure, Pete. If I'm frightened in big planes I don't see how flying in little planes will help."

"Well suit yourself," Pete replied with a hint of sarcasm. "I think you would have a lot of fun, and I'm sure it would help your fear of flying."

"If you are sure it will help, then I'll do it," I responded somewhat sceptically.

Pete arranged a convenient date and time for the both of us, and we were set to fly out of an airfield at High Wycombe. It was supposed to be half way between us, but I had to drive at least twice as far as he did. Still, I was not in a position to argue since I was about to put my life in his hands.

It was a beautiful day for flying: dry, a little wind, and very good visibility. Pete disappeared for about 10 minutes, apparently to sort things out with whomever was in charge of the airfield. We rented a Piper Cherokee for two hours and walked all around the plane as Pete inspected the exterior of the plane. I found this a bit disconcerting, thinking that someone should have already done this before we arrived. Why was Pete so worried anyway? It seemed to me that he was more frightened of flying this thing than I was at this point.

We circled the plane for a second time, and he told me the function each part of the plane played while flying. He explained the aerodynamics of the wings, which gives the plane lift when it reaches a certain speed. Then he explained that his first check of the plane was a procedure all pilots, even on commercial flights, are required to carry out to ensure that the plane is airworthy.

We entered a small cockpit. Pete took the left seat, and I the right. It appeared that I had just as many instruments in front of me as he had in front of him, which made me feel quite important. He started the engine — yes, just one — and mumbled a few words.

"What?" I shouted, as the engine noise was a bit overpowering. He mumbled some more.

"What did you say?" I shouted even louder.

"There's no need to shout," Pete said calmly in a normal voice. "I was just talking to the tower through this microphone. It's a special microphone that allows me talk in a quiet voice."

"Oh, sorry. Well what did you tell him?" I demanded, wanting to learn as much as possible.

"Just needed permission to move to the runway."

"Oh, OK."

We arrived at the side of the grass runway when Pete did his mumbling thing again and moved onto the runway. For the first time on this trip I could now feel my heart beat. I was definitely anxious. Pete turned to me with one of his smiles, and I knew that he was thinking of something wicked.

"I just want you to lightly hold this control," he said, pointing to what looked like a broken steering wheel with the top and bottom bits missing. "This will give you a feel of what I'm doing as we take off and fly."

"OK," I said, thinking that was an interesting training technique.

He pushed the throttle forward, and we started moving down the runway. Then, to my utter astonishment, he calmly said, "When we reach a certain speed I will ask you to pull back on that control," pointing to the broken steering wheel.

"Oh no Pete. No, no, this was not....no Pete I can't. I don't know how, Pete!" my voice getting louder and louder.

As we were careering down the bumpy runway, Pete just looked at me, smiled, and calmly said, "Gently pull back now."

"No Pete, I don't know how to fly. You do it. I'll…I'll do it next time." I stuttered very nervously, thinking to myself that there wouldn't be a next time.

"I'm not going to do it, so you had better gently pull back on that stick now because we are running out of runway," Pete expressed commandingly.

Sure enough, the end was getting closer and closer. By this time, my knuckles were bleached white. I could feel that the palms of my hands were soaked with nervous sweat. I did what I was told and slowly pulled back the broken steering wheel, and the plane went up in the air!

"Wow!" was all I could muster in my excitement, both for flying the plane and not killing myself at the end of the runway. By this time I couldn't have cared less about killing Pete.

"You are doing very well," Pete said calmly, "but you need to steer a little to the right to avoid that plane in front of us." I turned the control to the right, and sure enough, the plane took a right turn.

"Perfectly executed," I proudly said to Pete, as I was now on the verge of beginning to relax.

"Next time you make a turn you need to give the plane some rudder. Turn to the right, give it right rudder. Turn to the left, left rudder."

"Now don't get technical with me," I asserted. Actually it wasn't very technical at all. The rudder is operated by the foot bar and stops the plane sliding sideways, I think. I did what I was told, and the plane seemed to turn corners better.

We — actually I — had been flying for about 10 minutes when Pete said, "Where do you want to go?"

"First of all, where the hell are we?" since I had not paid any attention to the direction in which we were flying.

"I have no idea," Pete remarked jokingly, "how about we go to Silverstone."

That was fine with me since I had no better idea. I knew Silverstone from the ground — it's where I often watched the British Grand Prix, and the Johns (Bamford & Burton) had also done some sports car racing there.

When we attained an altitude of 2,000 feet, Pete told me to level off. We reached Silverstone, did a couple of pretend laps of the racetrack in the air, and then turned around and started back home. Up until this point Pete had allowed me to fly the plane, which really did help my confidence. It was also enjoyable. He then suggested that he take over, and we practice an emergency landing. My heart skipped a couple beats.

"An emergency landing?" I questioned anxiously.

"Yup" Pete answered lazily. "I always practice emergency landings when I'm on a trip like this. What I want you to do, Bamford, is to shut off the engine by pushing this lever all th..."

As his first words began to sink in, I never let him finish the sentence. "Shut off the engine!" I squealed in a high-pitched voice. "You must think I'm stark raving mad. There is no way in HELL I'm going to shut off anything, especially the engine of this plane."

As I was ranting away, the drone that had been with us for the last hour suddenly stopped. All went quiet except the hissing of the wind. My heart started pounding again like never before. Pete, in a peak of madness, had shut down the engine. Actually it was still idling. The plane was pointing downwards, and Pete was looking all around.

"I think we will land in that field there," he announced, pointing to a large green field.

"But there are some large pylons and high tension wires running across that field," I remarked quietly not knowing what to think or say at this point.

"Oh yeah, so there are. Well, we will land in that field then. Thanks for pointing that out Wally," Pete said matter-of-factly, using my old school nickname that I have always hated.

We took a steep dive toward the chosen field and levelled off over the field at a height of about 10 feet. "We would have made a good landing," Pete declared. As he pushed the throttle lever forward we began to climb, and my heart rate began to drop.

That was enough flying for one day. For many days in fact. Naturally, Pete landed the plane and when safely on the ground, I had to admit to him that it was an experience, a good learning experience.

"Do you want to come up again?" Pete asked, "You'll enjoy it much more the second time, as you will know what to expect."

"That's a very good reason not to go again, but on the other hand 'you only live once'," I reasoned. So we agreed to do it all over again and a new date and time were set. "I must be insane," I thought to myself as I drove back home.

The phone rang, and it was Pete to remind me that we had scheduled another flight together for tomorrow.

"Oh no, I hadn't forgotten," I said, which was the truth. I had been worrying about it for some days. At the allotted hour we met up at the same airfield in High Wycombe. This time we had a Cessna, with the wings above the cockpit. This was an advantage over the Piper Cherokee because one can see substantially more on the ground, however it didn't look as safe. The wings of the Cessna were held onto the fuselage by relatively small struts, which made the plane look a little delicate.

I knew what to expect after my first flight, and both Pete and I examined the exterior of the plane. I was a little apprehensive when we climbed into the cockpit, but I had previously asked Pete not to surprise me on the runway like he did on my first flight. I was more than happy to fly the plane once we were in the air, but it was his responsibility to handle the takeoff. He told me that was fine with him, which was a huge relief to me.

We taxied out to the same runway, same as last time, and he did his mumbling bit again. We stayed where we were as we watched another plane land. We were still pulling onto the runway when Pete pushed the throttles forward. The plane started bouncing down the grass runway.

Pete looked at me, and I gave him one incredible stare. He was sitting in the pilot's seat with his arms crossed. "You know how to fly this thing, so do everything I taught you last time," he said nonchalantly.

"You bastard," I yelled as the plane continued to gather speed. "You promised me you wouldn't do this to me."

"I made no such promise," Pete said, as he sat with his arms crossed.

I could tell he was serious, so I had to be as well. My hands grabbed the controls, and my knuckles instantly became white as I wrapped my fingers tightly around the handles and very gently pulled back, as I did last time. Much to my amazement the plane gently lifted off the ground. I don't know why I was so surprised, perhaps it was because I knew I really did do it all by myself. I worked all the controls as Peter had shown me last time, and we set course for Worcestershire to look at Picklewell and Upper Birch to take some photographs from the air.

Now full of confidence, we returned to the airfield, and Pete suggested I land the plane. He agreed to talk me through it, and I felt chuffed that he felt that I could do it. Pete did all the navigation and had all the contact with the control tower. He set me up on the approach and told me my speed and the height I needed to be. Other things needed to be attended to such as flaps, wind direction, and what seemed like a thousand other things.

"Bamford you are too high, get the plane down lower," Pete suggested.

"OK."

"Peter you are approaching much too fast, slow down," Pete stated.

"OK."

I slowed down and went lower as the runway was fast approaching.

"Wally slow down and get lower!" Pete said anxiously, "lower and slower, now!"

I was trying to do what he wanted me to do but somehow it wasn't coming together. Peter grabbed his broken steering wheel and commandingly said, "I'm taking control of the plane," at the point where we were about 15 feet above the runway and a little off course.

Rather rude of him I thought, taking over like that, but he was the captain.

We landed safely and were taxiing off the runway when Pete remarked, "you made a real cods whollop of that didn't you?"

"I don't think so," I replied, "we were 15 feet up, and we would have made a good landing," remembering his words when we practised making an emergency landing. We both chuckled and went off to have a pint or three in the local pub.

CHAPTER 17

SUPERNATURAL ENCOUNTERS

Upper Birch was a large house with expansive rooms, and we loved to entertain. We had numerous dinner parties, children's parties, and other larger parties like New Year's Eve, and once a large barbecue party. All of our guests seemed to enjoy themselves as much as we did.

The dining room was especially good for entertaining. It was large with a flagstone floor and a shoulder high stone fireplace. The stairway led from the dining hall to upstairs. At one end of the dining room there was a bay window with glass-in-lead windows and an archway leading to the kitchen at the other end. It was somewhat baronial in a modern setting, rather unusual with its flagstone floor. We heard later that not everyone shared our enthusiasm for our home. Some felt it was cold and uninviting and others just had a strange feeling about it.

At one of our dinner parties we invited some cousins — Edward with his wife, Oonagh and Betty with her husband, William. Suzan and I always sat at the end of the table with Suzan nearest to the kitchen. Betty and Edward sat with their backs to the fire facing the stairway facing William and Oonagh, with their backs to the stairs. Suzan had cooked another wonderful meal, which was really remarkable for someone who had never even ventured into the kitchen until she came to England. You would have to know Suzan's mother to understand why she never even made tea. When we were first married I was astounded to learn of her inability to cook and tried to show her the basics of the culinary art. That kind gesture was met with an angry onslaught, and I was summarily kicked out of the kitchen. I wasn't allowed back in for about 10 years, which was unfortunate since I enjoy cooking and am reasonably good at it.

We had a very pleasant evening with our cousins, nothing out of the ordinary, just a couple of cocktails and some good red wine. As my cousins lived about an hour away they came in one car. It was on the way home that Betty asked the other three whether they had noticed anything strange while they were at our house.

"You mean you also saw it!" exclaimed Edward.

"Yes," said Betty in very excitedly. "It was an apparition that floated out of the kitchen along the wall and up the staircase," finished Edward.

"That's exactly what happened," said both Betty and Edward to the other two, who by now were sitting with their mouths wide open and chills going down their back. Naturally with their backs to the staircase William and Oonagh were unable to see anything.

Edward, whom I have no reason to disbelieve other than that I have a hard time believing in apparitions or ghosts, relayed this story to Suzan and me some time later. He also said that Betty was one of those people who had "feelings" about certain houses, and she said our house had a strange feel about it. Naturally we were oblivious to this "sighting" and had no reason to believe that the house was haunted.

With Rozango docked at Lymington, a two and a half hour drive away, I tried to enjoy it as much as possible. Unfortunately my penchant for sailing was not matched by Suzan. She always felt that there was too much to do in the garden, the dogs had to be taken care of, and that Debbie was still a baby, all of which were true. But that was just an excuse, for any true enthusiast could easily overcome these problems: hire a gardener, put the dogs in kennels, and take Debbie with us. Fortunately Suzan is not a jealous woman at all and was quite happy for me to go sailing on the weekend.

It was on one such sailing weekend that Suzan was alone in the house with Debbie. She wasn't afraid of living there alone, and we had two neighbours about a quarter of a mile down the road that could help her out if there was a problem. The dogs were in their kennels for the night, which were some distance from the house. It was a Saturday night when Suzan decided to stay up late to work on the curtains in our bedroom. She had turned off all the lights downstairs, not anticipating having to go there again. Around one o'clock in the morning she realised she needed a pair of scissors from downstairs. As she walked past Debbie's room on the upper landing she suddenly heard the most terrible crashing sound, no cries of pain, just a heavy tumbling sound. According to her it sounded like a man falling down the stairs from top to bottom and then a heavy thud as he hit the solid oak front door. Suzan, a woman not easily scared, rushed back into the bedroom and called the police, who told her to stay put in the bedroom, and they would be out there shortly.

Three police cars arrived very quickly, without announcement, and surrounded the house. They approached the house from all sides to block off any escape and then, as prearranged with the police, Suzan opened the front door when she saw their car lights just below her bedroom. There was no body on the floor or any marks on the walls of the staircase to show that someone had fallen down. As the police continued a thorough search of the house and found no forced points of entry or exit and nobody in the house, Suzan was beginning to feel very embarrassed.

"I am very sorry to bring you all the way out here," Suzan said to the three officers. "You must think I'm an easily frightened and neurotic woman." Suzan is many things to many people but an easily frightened neurotic woman she is not.

"No, on the contrary we are glad to be able to help you out. Being alone at night can be frightening, especially in a large house," one of the officers commented.

"I definitely heard something loud. I just cannot think what it was."

The police radios crackled, and the police left in a hurry to tend to a rare shooting in Kidderminster.

When I arrived home from my weekend of sailing, Suzan started to relay the events of Saturday night. I have a hard time believing in ghosts, but this tale sent chills down my back. There was no other explanation. She had also heard the back door ring a couple of times and when she went to see who it was, there was no one there. With the body falling-down-the-stairs incident and the bell-ringing incident there was evidence building that perhaps the house was haunted — without even knowing about my cousins' experience. Suzan carried out an investigation to determine if a death had occurred in the house or other reason to make the house haunted. She came up with nothing.

In every room of the house there was a bell to summon the staff in days gone by. In the morning room, where the staff were presumably situated, there was a box on the wall that indicated in which room or door the bell had been rung. Our living room was huge, so often we would spend our evenings together in the morning room. One night, the box on the wall buzzed, indicating that there was someone at the back door, as it had done when Suzan was there alone. Suzan immediately stood up and went to see who it was. Again, she opened the door only to find no one there. This happened several nights in a row. I heard them all, so I knew that Suzan was not hallucinating. Sometimes I would go to the door, and sometimes Suzan would take a look. Each time the same thing occurred — no one was there. We thought it was some youths playing a prank on us, but we were not amused.

I had a brilliant idea. I smeared a thin coat of butter over the push button of the bell. This way, not only could I determine that there was somebody ringing the bell but I would also get his or her fingerprint! The next bell-ringing incident produced no fingerprint.

Then Suzan had a wonderful idea: we would send the dogs after them. Bloodhounds are renowned for their sense of smell and, if nothing else, they would scare the hell out of them. Normally the dogs had been put to bed by the time these events were happening, but we decided to keep them in until the next "ringing." Sure enough, it happened that night, and Suzan rushed the dogs to the back door. She pushed them outside where they just stood looking at her not knowing what they were supposed to do or what she was expecting of them — I know the feeling. Obviously nobody was there, so who was ringing the bell?

We surmised that perhaps it was some mice nibbling at the wires, but that wouldn't explain why it happened on a regular basis at roughly the same time of night. We both knew what the other was thinking but didn't dare mention it. But eventually the word ghost crept into the conversation.

"Ah no," I said quietly. "It couldn't be." I don't believe in that supernatural stuff. Nevertheless, to give us peace of mind, we decided to install an alarm system, even though I don't believe ghosts set off alarm systems. Anyway, the house was rather isolated, and we were concerned about burglaries. But the amazing thing is that soon after the installation, we noticed that the bell ringing stopped as quickly as it had started.

Suzan had several more minor "sightings" in the house, but I never saw anything. Although I thought that Suzan might have had strong feelings that the house was haunted, there was someone who absolutely felt a presence in the house.

We heard about an Argentinean girl looking for an au pair position to help out for about three months, as the family she was currently with was most unpleasant. Sounds familiar doesn't it? Since Suzan had a fair amount of work on her hands, we thought it agreeable to have Marga help out. She was a charming young girl, not much younger than we were. She was actually Yugoslavian, but had lived in Argentina for many years. She spoke

Spanish at home, and her English was very broken. Suzan and I both loved to hear her talk in her strong Spanish accent and tried our best to teach her English.

Marga had a small bedroom at the opposite end of the house from our bedroom. Marga's room was part of the original house, which we were told was over 300 years old. She was a religious girl, and we thought nothing of it when she asked us for some candles. Suzan only asked her to be careful with them, and Marga told us not to worry, as she would place them in the basin in her bedroom.

Marga left our house almost as quickly as she arrived. She told us that she had found another family in the London area where there was more to do. She said she was bored living in the country and wanted to enjoy the city life. I wasn't upset, more put out since I enjoyed having her around, and she was very good with Debbie. It wasn't until sometime later that Suzan told me about the candles.

"Aha, that's it!" I said to Suzan feeling like Sherlock Holmes, "she had the candles to ward off the spirits."

It wasn't so much that Marga was bored, but she felt she had to get out of the house — fast. She never let us know if she saw a ghost or whether she just felt that the house was haunted. We certainly never discussed our previous experiences with her, so whatever feelings she had were of her own making.

PART 4
A NEW START

CHAPTER 18

TIME TO RELOCATE

After leaving Touche Ross my business ventures were mostly unsuccessful. My partner at Thompson and Bamford was intolerable, a nonstop jabbering box with a huge ego. And a venture into the wine importing business with two French partners proved to be a "not for profit" organisation! The year of 1976 was a pivotal year. I finished winding up the affairs of André Guillaume, the wine company, and was out looking for something else to do. I needed a steady income.

One decision I made was to join Lloyds of London, the renowned insurance market. It was best known for its shipping insurance but covers all types of risks.

I was considering several types of businesses including a garden nursery from our home at Upper Birch or perhaps opening a wine bar, which were becoming popular. With my newly acquired knowledge of the wine industry, the wine bar seemed to be the best fit. I had a very good site in mind. It was an old building on the main street of Hagley, an affluent area close to Birmingham. The building had just the right ambience for a wine bar and had been vacant for some time. When I approach the powers that be about acquiring a license and opening a wine bar, the idea was flatly rejected.

I also found a vacant site on the Hagley Road in Birmingham, a main artery into the city. I felt the location was ideal to use as a retail outlet for the plants and shrubs that could be grown in our nursery at Upper Birch. The site was owned by British Rail and was located next to a disused railway line. Again, this was the perfect location for this type of business: it was on a busy road in a well-to-do area. When I approached British Rail, they would neither sell nor lease the site.

Both ideas came to an abrupt halt. Maybe, if I had invested a great deal of time and money I could have moved the authorities in my direction. The problem was that although I had the time, I didn't have the necessary funds to go through with it. At that time in England, income and corporate taxes were at a particularly high level. So, in the event that the business was successful (which was certainly not guaranteed), the amount of net income received after tax was not commensurate with the risks being taken.

I concluded that I should abandon all ideas of starting my own business and look for employment. I started scouring the newspapers and accountancy journals for something suitable. I was a 29-year-old with a good professional designation and experience in both private practice and industry. When I found something suitable, the salary being offered was pitiful even before taxes were deducted. How was I going to bring up my children and send them to good schools on that salary? How was I going to keep up the standard of living that I had come accustomed to? The only way that this seemed possible was to use the capital that I had invested: not a good idea! I could see many of my friends struggling with the same problems, and even those who had their own businesses were having a hard time.

At the same time the political events in the United Kingdom were terrible. The Labour government had been in power for some time, hence the high taxes. Many of the government's decisions were based on very strong union input since the unions were, in general, financing the Labour Party. Strikes were rampant including train strikes, transportation strikes, and coal miner's strikes. Power disruptions, brown outs and black outs, were common. We kept candles and equipment to boil water and cook food. While all this was going on inflation was raging around 18 percent. What a mess. I really couldn't see how things could be turned around. The so-called "brain drain" had been steadily going on for some years. These were mainly professional people, doctors, professors, accountants etc. who were emigrating to North America for considerably higher salaries and a better living standard. In the meantime, everyone in the British colonies at that time was entitled to a British passport. However bad I felt about Britain, to these colonials, Britain was paradise with its National Health Service, good accommodation, and for them, excellent paying jobs. So what happened was many of the well-educated British citizens left, while many more uneducated British passport holders from the colonies were streaming into the country. With all this churning around in my unsettled mind, I decided it was time to make a move, a major move!

I nervously laid out my plan to Suzan. I had no idea how she would react to the idea of emigrating. I explained my thought process and how hopeless the situation seemed in England. I told her of my concern for the children's education and how strongly I felt about making a break from everything. I really couldn't explain this part of my reasoning, but it was just a strong feeling within me. Fortunately, Suzan concurred. She had already made a break from her family ties in Holland and didn't feel that moving again would affect them too badly. Wherever we went, it was still a plane flight away. Of course, the downside to this whole idea was leaving my family and our friends. However you look at this, there were always pros and cons. But that was it. We made our decision.

Now there was a big question in both of our minds. Where in the world were we going to go — literally? As funny as this may sound, we got out a world atlas and started to look. With my language skills there was no way I was going to go to a non-English speaking country. That still left us with a good variety to choose from. Suzan said she didn't want to go to Australia or New Zealand because they were too far away from Holland and England. That basically left South Africa, the United States and Canada. We felt that places like India, Hong Kong, and the many other English-speaking colonies to be unsuitable. Even though we understood that South Africa is a beautiful country, the political situation was volatile and unacceptable. That left the United States and Canada. We learned that the

United States was a difficult country to obtain immigration papers for, but because Canada is a part of the British Commonwealth, it was considerably easier. In my investigation about the country I came to the conclusion it was a "have all" country. It is the second largest country in the world after Russia with a population close to 30 million. It has huge resources of minerals, timber, and farmland. Canadian lifestyles tend to be healthy and their crime rate is low. It seemed to us the best place to start a new life — but where in Canada.

It was now time to tell my mother of our plan. Much to my surprise she took it very much in stride and said that she thought we might be thinking of moving. As we approached New Year's Eve, we decided to have a big New Year's party. As usual, no one was doing anything; consequently we had a great turnout. We knew that it was going to be our last party at Upper Birch, so we put all our effort into making it a memorable one. Good food, good company. A beautifully decorated house and a plentiful flow of all types of drinks. It was here, at this black-tie event, that we announced our plans to emigrate. All of them felt that we were doing the right thing. (Maybe they weren't such good friends after all!) The encouragement we received from them removed any doubts I had about our plan.

My trip to Canada was a 10-day trip with the idea of visiting as many cities as possible to ascertain the job market in each and determine whether that city would be a good place to live and bring up children. I flew to Toronto in January, which I felt was a good month to test my stamina for the cold. If I liked Canada in January then surely I would like it the rest of the year. My British Airways flight was supposed to take me to Toronto, however the city was enduring the worst snowstorm it had had in many years, so our flight was diverted to Chicago. When I eventually arrived in Toronto, snow was piled high; I thought this was normal. One of my bags was missing, which I knew was not normal. On the airport bus to my hotel we were preceded by three snowplows, one in each lane, going down Queen Elizabeth Highway. Very clever I thought; this must be the way it is done. After what seemed to be an interminable drive, we reached my hotel close to the centre of the city. By this time I was famished, so I went to the bar to see if I could get something to eat. "Kitchen's closed," came back the reply. At the end of the bar there were about 20 men seemingly having a good time after being stranded by the snowstorm. One man was crying on another man's shoulder and a couple of other men were a little close to each other. Maybe this is not so normal I thought, but I was still rather naïve.

I went to bed at 1 a.m., 6 a.m. in England, and crashed. Before I went to sleep I tried to sum up my day. It was my first transatlantic crossing, I unexpectedly went to the United States, where I spent four hours on the plane; the airline had lost my luggage; I had arrived in Toronto immediately after the biggest snowstorm they had experienced in decades; and then I checked into a gay hotel where they weren't serving any food. I was asleep before I could draw any conclusions.

The next morning, after a hearty English breakfast, I wandered outside where the sun was shining brightly in a deep blue sky. It felt very refreshing after leaving England on a damp, dreary day. The city was getting itself going again with snowplows, salt trucks and ice melters, which seemed to leave tons of water on the road side as the drainage system couldn't handle it. As I was standing on the pavement taking in all the sights and smells, a large truck came trundling by with the name BAMFORD painted in large letters on the side. This has to be a good omen I thought.

The cars were huge by European standards, and the sound of the V8 engines rumbling away at the traffic lights reminded me of the highly tuned racing engines in the Class I power boats. It was exciting to see all the skyscrapers and the newly completed CN Tower, the world's tallest freestanding structure. The city was vibrant and proud with new office buildings under construction and their newly completed Metro underground rail system. It was interesting to see that as many as seven city blocks were connected underground, full of stores and eating establishments. These areas were well-trafficked, especially during the winter months.

I interviewed with Touche Ross to see what jobs they may have available. They were somewhat interested in me for their bankruptcy department, especially since I had just finished winding up the affairs of André Guillaume. Unfortunately, they needed someone immediately, and at that time I hadn't even applied for immigration papers. So they said for me to call when I was living in Toronto. I looked at job opportunities in the papers, and there seemed to be plenty with salaries at about 30 to 40 percent higher than back home. I was excited about the possibilities of living here. House prices seemed a little on the high side, but with a higher salary this should not prove to be too much of a problem.

I felt that I needed to check out Montreal, although the language issue would probably be a problem. Montreal has a true cosmopolitan feel about it, with people from many parts of the world living there. It had a genuine European flavour with its small boutique shops, high fashion, and smaller streets. The restaurants, of course, were wonderful. Both English and French was spoken there, but French was definitely the predominant language. I had no problem getting around, but to work there you really need to be bi-lingual.

Rather than flying to Montreal, I decided to take the train. I had heard it was a high-speed train with all the latest technology. It was slightly cheaper than a flight, and as with most train services, drops you off in the centre of the city. Outbound, the service was very efficient, comfortable, and even had viewing decks to give you a panoramic view of the scenery. I also enjoyed the dining car and the drink service. Things were not so good on the return trip. About halfway into the trip, the train came to an abrupt halt. Some of the passengers in my section advised me that this was not an unusual event at this time of the year. Apparently, the train had been designed in California, where they neglected to account for the very cold weather. After about an hour I could feel the temperature starting to drop in the carriage. Eventually a VIA rail official came through our section and announced that they had a problem with the train. What a stunning announcement, I thought sarcastically, having sat there for a couple of hours watching blue uniformed men walking up and down the tracks. He went on to say that the train's hydraulic system that worked the train's suspension was broken, which would make the ride very bumpy from now on. Because of this, the train would not be able to travel at high speeds but the good news was that the heating system would work to some degree when the train started moving again. It would take some time to reach Toronto, but if we wished, they would allow us to get off the train and make our own way. I looked out of the window to see where we were, and all I could see was snow covered scrubland — not a house or a building in sight! It was a crazy suggestion, which naturally no one accepted. They were right in their assessment. It was a bumpy ride, so bumpy that I could not write on the table in front of me. The train did heat up a bit, but not enough to take off my coat. Finally the train arrived four and a half hours late in Toronto. All of us had had enough and crowded to the exit doors. And there we stood, two minutes, five minutes, seven minutes, but the doors wouldn't open. Finally, another official came to our door and explained that the doors were operated by the train's hydraulic system and that they were going to open each door manually. What a fitting end to a miserable "high-tech" train ride.

So far, I had determined that Canada would be a great place to settle and that Toronto would be a good place to live. However, I had a stock question that I asked of everyone I met. This would include people with whom I interviewed, people I struck up conversations in the bars, and people on the train. In fact almost everyone I talked to during the whole trip. The question was: "If you were me and had the choice to move to any city in Canada to work and live, where would you go?"

At that time Manitoba, Ontario, Quebec, and all the eastern provinces were experiencing a recession. However, British Columbia had a steady economy, and Alberta was in the middle of its greatest boom. This was almost entirely due to their oil and gas industry. North of Edmonton there are huge deposits of tar sands which they now had the technology to convert to oil, and they were also finding many regular oil fields. Drilling had hit a feverish pitch, and there were many times that they would find a natural gas field when drilling for oil. Most of the heavy industrial companies connected with the oil and gas industry were based out of Edmonton, and the company headquarters and finance companies were based in Calgary.

So invariably, when I asked my question, about 80 percent of them replied Calgary and the other 20 percent said they would go to Vancouver because the weather there was much milder. Next stop, Calgary.

On the approach to Calgary airport, if you are lucky enough to have a window seat, you get a wonderful view of the city nestled against the Rocky Mountains to the west and the end of the prairies on its east side.

Calgary looked and felt different from any other city I had visited. In 1977 it was a city that was coming of age. The Calgary Stampede was still the major tourist attraction, and the surrounding farmland still had many cattle ranches. However, high finance and large commercial office buildings were supplementing the western feel to the town. Its rapid growth and newfound wealth produced an air of excitement, and I wasn't about to let that feeling slide by. I inhaled all the facts and figures that I could. In January the weather was bloody freezing, but the sky was mostly a deep blue colour and the sun shone brightly. It was an exhilarating feeling. As usual, I walked the length and breadth of the city, talking to as many people as possible and taking in the sights. I visited Banff about one hour from Calgary in the Rocky Mountains. The drive out was exciting. As you leave Calgary behind, heading west, the scenery is rather bland with rough, flat pasture land that belonged to the natives. Then there is a point where you start to climb, and suddenly as you round a bend you see the majestic Rockies in the distance. They are very stark, beautiful, and dramatic as they rise out of the plains. Naturally, in January there were snow-covered mountains, and the ski resorts were in full swing. I love to ski, but my financial situation kept me from participating. However, by this time I had made up my mind that Calgary is where I would like to settle. The job situation appeared better than anywhere else, the city was dynamic and economically stable, and with the mountains so close by there was endless recreation — I just loved the place! With this decision in my pocket there didn't seem to be any reason to go on to Vancouver. By all accounts it was a beautiful city, but the economy was not as good, and the weather was very similar to that in England. After being in Calgary with its bright sun, if not cold days, I didn't relish the thought of the many rainy and cloudy days I would endure in Vancouver.

CHAPTER 19

CANADA, EH!

Obtaining our immigration papers was a relatively simple affair. A young, married professional with two children was exactly what the Canadian immigration office was looking for. They were not concerned that I was going without a job, especially since I had chosen Calgary to live. We sold Upper Birch, which to me was truly heart breaking, and set the date for my departure. Suzan and the children were to stay at my mother's until I had found a job. The family gave me a wonderful "surprise" going away party at Neenie and James's house and invited all of our friends. My mother gave me some very assuring words, letting me know that if things didn't work out in Canada there was always a place for me at home. And that was it.

I had a direct flight from London Heathrow to Calgary. I was a new immigrant, so I had to be processed; I went from one department to another. Questions were asked, records checked, papers stamped, all on top of a nine-hour flight. Nothing like Ellis Island I am sure, but still an ordeal. Since there were only two of us going through the procedure, we had the attention of their whole department. Finally, I received the one big blue stamp I needed in my passport, and I was on my way — to collect my luggage. When I arrived at the baggage handling area for my flight, not only was there no one around, but there were no bags. That's sensible, I thought. They have taken my luggage to their office to prevent someone else from taking it. A check at the office revealed nothing. An official declared that my suitcase was probably left on the plane and was on its way to Vancouver. I was irritable, fed up, and tired. Two trips to Canada and twice my luggage had been lost!

"So what are you going to do about it," I demanded, thinking maybe I should have chosen Vancouver after all.

"We are very sorry about this sir, where are you staying?" the official answered in a calm and pleasant voice. The official's demeanour took me by complete surprise, as I was not use to this pleasant approach.

"At the Holiday Inn," I replied.

"We'll have your bags delivered first thing in the morning".

True to their word, the suitcase was delivered to my room first thing. What a relief. After a day and a half in the suitcase, I felt the clothes should be unpacked immediately. I opened the top, and to my utter astonishment the first thing I saw was one, blue satin high heel, size six shoe! Strange people these Canadians.

Now I had my work cut out, as I had to find a job and somewhere to live on a temporary basis. I couldn't stay at the Holiday Inn forever. Obviously the job was the first order of business. Even though I had a good accounting qualification from England, I came to Calgary with the attitude that I was prepared to take any job at first and then work my way up the company. I knew I could do it; all I needed was a chance. I went to several interviews but with no success. I was beginning to feel that my strong English accent might have something to do with it, but now I don't think that was the case. I scoured the papers every day and made many calls. It had now been a month of job searching and I was becoming a somewhat despondent. I signed up with the "executive" search firm Robert Half, who specialised in accounting positions. Not having a support group of friends or business associates made things worse. It was at this time I made a serious promise to myself. The company that hired me would receive from me a total commitment, my maximum energy and ability so long as they wanted me.

I telephoned Suzan to find out how she and the children were doing. They were all fine and then she stunned me saying that they had booked a flight to Calgary on 7-7-77. This was an easy date to remember when she emigrated, she thought.

"But I don't even have a job yet," I protested, but she seemed determined. It was my plan, and it seemed financially sensible for the children and her to stay in England until I had found a job. But if you knew Suzan, you would realise that I had lost the debate before it even had started. July 7th it would be and given my deteriorating mental state, it was probably a good thing.

I was looking forward to seeing them all when she called the day before her trip to let me know that Jeremy had bronchitis and wasn't allowed to travel. It didn't sound too bad but it stopped everyone coming until a few days later.

Fortunately I had found somewhere to live. With two children and Basil the bloodhound, it was not an easy task. Many apartments didn't want children and nearly all of them didn't allow pets. I eventually found a house that was perfect. The owner had developed the downstairs area and he and his family were living there. They had a separate entrance, so consequently there was never a problem of living on top of each other. They didn't seem to be concerned that we had a big dog or the children, so I took it immediately. Mind you, I don't think they were aware how big a dog I was bringing into their house.

There was a problem that I needed to resolve as soon as possible: Before I left England, I had made myself a package of female clothing and jewelry and mailed it to my hotel. After a couple of weeks, I checked at the front desk on a daily basis. No package. After I moved out I checked at the hotel on a weekly basis and then on a monthly basis, still no package. Six months later there was the package. Apparently I hadn't put sufficient postage on the parcel, and it had come by sea!

I rented a car to pick everyone up from the airport. They all seemed in very good spirits, even after a long flight. Basil, who had been drugged by a special veterinary service at Heathrow airport, had come around, but was still very groggy. For the flight he had to have a special box made, and the cost for him, which goes by the pound, was almost as much as an adult fare.

That morning, Robert Half called to say that a real estate company was looking for an assistant controller, and he thought I would be a good fit. An appointment was made for my interview the next day. At the time I didn't know what a real estate company was or what an assistant controller did!

On Wednesday I had the interview with Trizec, a large Canadian real estate company. Of course I was extremely nervous, but the controller, Glen Murray, immediately put me at ease. He and his wife had just returned from a trip to England, which thankfully they really enjoyed. We chatted for about an hour, and at the end he asked to come back in the afternoon to meet with the division's Vice-President. I was elated. The job was at the right level given my experience. It was in an industry, commercial property management and development, that I had a strong interest in, and if I got the job I would be working for someone I felt was a caring person and from whom I could learn. My interview with the Vice-President went well, so I was hired at an annual salary of Can$24,000. At the time, this was considerably more than I could have earned in England. It seemed that Suzan's intuition was right.

With a job in hand, we felt it was time to find a home of our own. We went looking with an agent but didn't see anything that was remotely interesting. I knew we were going to take a huge step down from Upper Birch, but these houses were unacceptable.

One major hurdle we faced was that the British government didn't allow anyone to take more than £5,000 out of the country. I had plenty of assets in England that I hoped to use as collateral for a down payment on a house. I had also bought a brand new Porsche 924, left-hand drive, tax-free, which was being shipped out with our furniture. I bought the car sight unseen but felt, being a Porsche, it would be just fine. The idea was that if I needed money I would sell the car — maybe.

On Friday, I felt that I needed to get Suzan a car so I went to a Chrysler dealership — why Chrysler I don't know. I selected what seemed to me to be a large station wagon and filled out all the paperwork to buy it on credit. Credit denied came back the reply.

"Credit denied? What do you mean, I have excellent credit!"

I hate buying cars. I always feel that I am being cheated.

"No, I am sorry sir, you don't have any credit history in Canada, and therefore we can't sell you this car on credit," the salesman announced rather aloofly.

"Well of course I don't have any credit history in Canada. I have only been here a month!" I reasoned. But it was to no avail, so I left in disgust.

Well, I will buy a used car, I concluded. It's a much better investment anyway. I looked at a few car lots, but none of the cars had any prices on them. Coming from England this seemed to be a very strange practice. I didn't know the value of these cars, and they weren't advertising them. The salesmen could see me coming a mile away. I knew I was getting the run around on the cost, and I was getting very disheartened. Then, by chance, I found a car lot with all the prices written clearly on the windscreen of each car. I looked around and found a car that really caught my eye. It was a dark green station wagon, a 1970 something Plymouth Grand Fury. This was it. We could get everybody, plus guests and the dog in this car. The price was Can$3,000, just what I could afford. I made inquiries, and the salesman/ owner promised it was in great mechanical condition!

"Can I drive it," I asked?

"Sure," came back the reply. He gave me the keys, and he didn't even want to come with me.

This is not normal in England. My mind was racing with the possibilities: Maybe I'll only get so far before it breaks down, and he didn't want to be stuck away from his business. Or worse still, maybe it's a stolen car. Or just maybe he is a nice person.

"I want to take the car to my wife to see if she likes it, is that alright?"

"Sure," he said not knowing where my wife lived.

It was wonderful to drive: a powerful V8 engine, power steering, power windows, power everything. The ride was very smooth, and there were no rattles. I loved the car but I was wondering how Suzan would react. Much to my amazement, after she had driven it she said she liked it too, even though it was enormous.

"Did you like it," the salesman asked when I returned?

"Sure," I replied feeling like a true Canadian.

I decided to buy the car and gave the man a check for Can$3,000, and with minimal paperwork the car was mine. I later learned that he was probably a happy salesman that night since I didn't carry out any bargaining. Oh well. I had acquired what proved to be a very reliable and comfortable car.

On Saturday, with a new-to-us car in hand, we followed our agent to a couple of houses. One looked promising, but was not perfect: we wanted a large dining room to place the antique dining room furniture we were bringing from England. Then she showed us a new house complete with carpets, brand new kitchen cabinets and appliances, and a view of the Rockies. The dining room was large enough for our antique dining furniture. There were five bedrooms and two full bathrooms, a living room, a family room, a two-car garage and a small garden. This was perfect. We put an offer in on the house, and it was accepted that day. We were ecstatic.

What an unbelievable week. Suzan, the children and Basil arrived on Tuesday, I secured a good job on Wednesday, acquired a new car on Friday, and we bought a new house on Saturday! We were all set for our new life in Canada.

CHAPTER 20

CAUGHT RED-HANDED

As time went on, nothing changed for me mentally. The female side of me was as present and strong as ever. There wasn't a day I didn't think about it, and I acted out my feelings whenever possible by dressing up or putting makeup on and doing my hair. In those days it was quite fashionable for young men to wear their hair long, so it was easy for me to have a female looking hairstyle when I wanted to. I am not sure if it was accidental or subliminally by design, but Suzan was just under 6 feet tall, and some of her clothes fit me quite well. Shoes however, have always been the bane of my life, as I have particularly wide feet. I have always found it difficult to find properly fitting shoes.

My depressions had been coming and going on a regular basis, and I didn't know if the two problems were related. Both were difficult to live with and added anxieties to my life. Thoughts of suicide had been with me since my teens but, even though I have been close to it, I had never felt so bad or so hopeless as to take my life.

We had been in Canada just over a year, and life was good for us as a family. I loved my job at Trizec and living adjacent to the Rockies, which became our playground during both the summer and winter, was a huge bonus. We had made a few friends, and although my work was challenging, life seemed relaxed. Almost every day we would start the day with a bright blue sky, something unfamiliar to an Englishman. Every day seemed to bring new sights, sounds, and smells: the roar of a steam during a spring runoff, the clean scented air of the Rockies, the evening smell of several BBQs fired up, the sight of constant new construction of skyscrapers. Despite all of this, there was also still the ever present personal problems I was facing.

As I readied myself for work one morning, Suzan was preparing breakfast and getting the children ready for school when she unexpectedly walked into the bedroom. I was momentarily stunned, frozen with fear. Tearfully, I went up to her and put my arms around her, and she reciprocated. We stood there for a while as she comforted me, and when I had calmed down she turned around and left. Few words were spoken — unusual for Suzan — but those that were, were by her and were reassuring. Her parting words were practical.

"Breakfast will be ready in a few minutes," she said.

What an amazingly strong woman I thought. I took off her panties and finished getting myself ready for work. I had fully intended to wear them that day.

I sheepishly arrived to have breakfast and said goodbye to the children as Suzan took them to school.

"Suzan!" I said, as she was hurriedly leaving.

As I struggled to find the right words, I continued "We'll chat about things tonight," and then she and the children were gone.

Driving to work, my mind was racing. Suzan seemed to take things very well, or had she? She didn't seem to be mad, but maybe she was seething and was keeping it in. What if she had decided to leave me! What if she and the children weren't there when I came back from work! Oh God! Wake me up from this nightmare.

Work that day was just a case of going through the motions. I couldn't concentrate; I felt physically sick all day and couldn't face lunch. What if Suzan decided to go public with her newfound knowledge and tell our friends, including Glen, my boss, and his wife Linda. Things at Trizec would never be the same. Oh Lord what am I going to do?

As my mind was twisting and turning and my thoughts became tangled, I remembered some prose by Max Ehrmann[5]

> Nurture strength of spirit to shield you in sudden misfortune.
> But do not distress yourself with dark imaginings.
> Many fears are born of fatigue and loneliness.
> Beyond a wholesome discipline,
> be gentle with yourself.

I felt lonely and realized that I needed to stop with the dark imaginings and start dealing with facts. And the fact was I didn't know what Suzan was thinking, and I needed to get home as soon as possible and talk with her.

Arriving home, I was very relieved to find Suzan's car in the garage. She appeared to be acting quite normal, and we all had dinner together as usual. After the children were in bed, feeling much less nauseated but with my stomach in knots, I turned the TV down and turned to Suzan and said,

"I am so sorry about this morning," emphasizing the word 'so'.

Looking a little surprised that I turned the TV down, Suzan said "Oh, that's OK, after 10 years I have become use to your depressions."

"Depressions!" I repeated loudly in a very startled manner. And not thinking clearly at all I continued, "You mean you didn't notice I was wearing your panties?"

---

5. Max Ehrmann, Desiderata, Copyright 1952.

"Wearing my panties?" she repeated quizzically. "No! I never noticed. I am so unobservant. So that's what all the fuss was about. It's not a big deal. If wearing my panties makes you feel better," Suzan continued in a matter-of-fact way, "I really don't mind."

"Oh!" I uttered in amazement. This was turning out so much better than I had imagined. But then I slowly realized that Suzan thought that I only had a fetish for women's underwear. How could she know differently?

Should I tell her the truth? Was this the time to come clean about all my feelings? I had thought about telling her before but had never had the courage, and in any case why risk ruining a very good relationship. On the other hand it didn't feel right keeping a secret in our marriage. I absolutely detest secrets, just as I detested living this lie. While these thoughts were running through my mind Suzan had turned the TV back up to continue watching whatever she had been watching before.

Having summoned up 'Dutch' courage with a couple of whiskies, I blurted out, "Suzan, I think you should know that I have always wanted to be a female."

"Oh", she responded slowly trying to absorb what I had just said. "I really don't mind."

She obviously did not comprehend the magnitude of my problem as I saw it. How could she? So I let it go at that, feeling very relieved having told her, but frustrated that I hadn't been able to properly convey my feelings.

Over the next few days, I managed to let Suzan know the extent of my transsexual feelings. She was sympathetic, but felt that there was nothing she could do. She later let me know that if I wanted to 'dress up', I could do it our bedroom, but she didn't want to see me. Without it being said, we both instinctively knew that the children would not be involved in any way.

So on occasions that varied in length of time, I would retreat to our bed-room and make myself look as female as possible. At least now I didn't have to be as exact when I put things away, and the constant fear of being dis-covered had been eliminated.

But none of this reduced my relentless and overwhelming desire to be fe-male. But I was not, and with the children still at a young age, it was out of the question. In any case I was now in my mid-30s and felt my chances for a complete change had gone. Why I thought that, I have no idea. It seemed that with the turning of every landmark year, my chances of doing anything had dissipated. First, it was just before I became a teenager and my voice broke, and then it was when I turned 21 and again when I turned 30. And even though the operation had become more prevalent and, thankfully, no longer forced to be carried out third world countries, it seemed to me, incorrectly I might add, that I was passed a suitable age to proceed.

CHAPTER 21

CANADIAN ENGLISH

Starting work at Trizec was rather intimidating. I really didn't know anything about real estate. The basic accounting principles were the same, but the business itself, the language, customs, and endless acronyms were all strange to me.

"Peder'" as my name was now pronounced, "Which credenza do you want in your office," Glen's secretary said to me.

"Oh, I'll let you know," I said in complete bewilderment not knowing what a credenza was. I scurried off to get a dictionary hoping to find the word "credenza" explained in English.

> Cre-den-za n. A buffet or sideboard, esp. one without legs. [Ital. < Med. Lat. *credentia*, trust, from the practice of placing food and drink on a sideboard to be tasted by a servant before being served to ensure that they contained no poison.]

Wow! Was I going to get a buffet or sideboard in my office? This couldn't be right, could it? So I went back to Glen's secretary.

"Excuse me," I said in my best English, feeling very foolish, "but what's a credenza?"

"Oh, it's the piece of furniture behind your desk, you know a credenza."

"Oh thanks," I said "I had never heard of that in England."

We both laughed and carried on with our work. This taught me a new lesson. Never worry about asking a question. Everyone is anxious to help, especially when you are new to a country.

Glen was extremely understanding and helpful. We got on very well, and he and his wife Linda became very good friends of ours. His work ethics were exemplary, and his attitude towards work always amused me. He was unconditionally an 8.30 a.m. to 5.00 p.m. man, which was unusual for a senior employee. He said that if you couldn't do you work in the allotted time that something was wrong. Either you couldn't handle the job or you needed extra help. This was not always true, especially at the end of a quarter when the accounting department had a great deal of extra work and no extra help. We had no desktop computers in those days; everything was done by hand. Most of the basic responsibility of producing the quarter end reports fell on the assistant controller. To get the work accomplished on time we often had to work long days. But Glen always left the office at 5:00 p.m.

"Good night!" he would say walking out of his office. "Now if you had worked hard during the day like me, you could be going home as well." We would all groan and get on with our work.

Glen was a mentor to me. He taught me to always be truthful, especially in business, so that you never had to think what story you told to whom. He taught me that nobody knows everything, so don't be afraid to admit it if you don't know something. He taught me to go back to basics to resolve a problem. I will always remember him drawing "T" accounts, the most basic of accounting practices, to work out how something should be done.

No other controller would dream of doing this. In doing so he taught us how to resolve a problem. Mistakes were rarely, if ever made. The accounting department in our region was deemed to be the best in the company. He taught me so many things and built up my confidence. I am grateful to him beyond words.

Although Canadians speak English, I learned that it was a different language to the one I spoke. On one occasion, Glen and I decided that we could manage with one less project accountant. Late in the day I called the unfortunate woman into my office and explained the situation, not a pleasant task. I told her that Glen or I would be happy to give her a good reference and she left. She cleared out her desk and told everyone what had happened. I felt like I needed to explain to rest of the group the circumstances, so I invited everyone to a local bar, where we went quite often after work. At an opportune moment I explained that I had to "let go" their colleague, as Glen and I felt that we had too many people and that her duties would be split up amongst the others. About a day later, Glen came to my office and explained that he had just been speaking to our ex-employee who said that I was spreading rumours about her being fired and was damaging her chances of being rehired in Calgary!

"I never said that," I said indignantly.

"Well she's madder than hell and plans to send a letter to the president," Glen explained, "but don't worry — it's all a storm in a teacup."

I went back to my group, which now consisted of three project accountants and an accounting manager and asked which one of them told the ex-employee that I had fired her. No one confessed, but it had to be one of them. She did write to the president and there was more discussion but it all blew over very quickly. It was only later that I found out the phrase "let go" in Canada (and the USA) means fired as opposed to "laid off." I didn't make that mistake twice.

CHAPTER 22

NEW NUANCES

Settling into our new home, finding our way around, and discovering Calgary was fun. Every day was an exciting challenge that I thrived on. To me, everything was so new that it seemed like an elongated holiday. Most days I would get up to a bright blue sky, even if the weather was well below freezing — it generally was from October through March. Sometimes, deep into the winter months, the temperature would get to -40°, which is that magical number where Fahrenheit meets Celsius. The air in Calgary is very dry, and they say that you don't feel the cold when the air is dry. That might be the case for a Canadian, but I can tell you that's not so for an Englishman. But even though it was so cold, it was a new experience. It's a strange feeling when you walk outside in such cold weather: the moisture in your nostrils freezes and there is a strange stillness in the countryside and undeveloped areas around where we lived.

The massive Rocky Mountains were due west of Calgary, and there was little else between the city and Vancouver at sea level. However this geographical situation produced an extraordinary phenomenon. The climate in Vancouver was mild, and occasionally during the winter months a westerly wind would push the warm Vancouver air over the Rockies. As the air started to ascend the temperature of the air would drop. When this cold air reached the eastern side of the Rockies, the air would descend and, in doing so, would warm up. Consequently, in the middle of a freezing winter,

Calgary would experience this warm wind called a Chinook. The effect was amazing. In the space of a few hours the temperature would rise from say minus 15º C to plus 15º C in just a few hours. Like a true Canadian I would take advantage of this by washing my salt-ravaged car, often with my shirt off. Normally this phenomenon lasted a couple of days at most, and within a few hours we were back to reality. It was said that this huge swing in temperatures often had an unsettling effect on some people, even to the point of suicide. To me it was just a nice reprieve.

It could snow in any month, but generally speaking the summer days were beautiful and warm. On trips to the mountains we always had our coats with us, and during the winter months we learned from the locals to always take a survival kit with us in the car. This homemade kit would include matches, a shovel, chocolate, string, an aluminum tray/dish for melting snow, and a candle. Since Calgary was at 3,500 feet above sea level the air was much thinner. This meant that Suzan had to adjust all of her recipes to take this into account especially when baking and cooking. We had a lot to learn, but it was fun.

When the snow really started to come in that first year we were astonished and excited to see that our house had the thickest and longest icicles in the neighbourhood. They were very beautiful, something that you never see in England. We were certainly very proud of them until, that is, one of our neighbours told us that large icicles were a symptom of poor insulation. He suggested we check to see how much insulation the builder had put in the roof. Much to our amazement, there was none. And we thought our gas bill was low! Our apologetic builder instantly rectified this, putting an end to our prize-winning icicles.

I was getting established at work and enjoyed every day I was there. Debbie was settling in at her new school, and Jeremy started play school two mornings a week. They were soon beginning to change their speech, especially their intimations of various words. Suzan and I were making new friends, hers mainly in the neighbourhood and mine at work. However, through my Aunt Pat back home, we became very good friends of Peter and Rosie Barling, who were both doctors. They lived in Canmore, located just outside Banff National Park. Canmore was once a small mining village that had the most beautiful and majestic mountains around it. We visited the Barling's often, had good old-fashioned English-style Sunday lunches with them and then drove home late Sunday night after a weekend of skiing in the winter or barbecuing in the backcountry in the summer. Normally Suzan would drive, I would fall asleep in the passenger seat, the kids would be fast asleep in the back seats, and Basil would be sleeping way in the back with our luggage stacked in front of him. A full load of snoring people and a dog to keep Suzan company.

Having doctors as friends is always a benefit, especially for the small, annoying ailments. Once while we were visiting Peter and Rosie I mentioned to Peter that I had a persistent and embarrassing rash in my groin area.

"Oh!" he said, "Come with me I can fix that."

I was somewhat taken aback as we jumped into his Jeep, with his huge black Newfoundland dog, and drove to his clinic just a few minutes away. I had no idea what he had in mind. We entered the surgery, and he took me through to the back area where he had dozens of samples of all types of different medicines. He rummaged through a few tubes and tablets and finally found what he was looking for.

Without even looking at the problem area he handed me a cream. "Here," he said with a smile on his face, "use this twice a day."

"Thank you," I murmured slowly wondering why Peter was smiling.

"Did I mention," Peter continued, "that you need to rub this cream between your toes!"

"Between my toes?" I quizzed him in astonishment. "But my problem is jock rash," I said blatantly.

"I know, I know, but just do as I say and your problem will be cured."

Well he was the doctor and even though I knew Peter to be a practical joker I didn't think he would fool around with his profession. So I did exactly as he prescribed and rubbed the cream between my toes twice a day. In the beginning, I could almost hear Peter laughing at me. But incredibly within 10 days my rash had completely disappeared never to return! It's amazing what these country doctors know.

The drinking and driving laws seemed a little stricter in Canada than in England at that time, and as a newcomer I certainly didn't want to get on the wrong side of the law. However, having said that, by Christmas time I still hadn't acquired an Alberta driver's license, nor had I changed the plates on my car from the "Z" plates from Germany to the Alberta number plates that include the required road tax. I wanted to make the changes, but time just flew by, and I never seemed to find the right moment. The issue was just not a high priority.

After an informal Christmas party with the accounting staff one evening, I found that I had partaken in a few more libations and a little less food than normal. So being somewhat concerned about driving home, especially at that time of year, I sensibly decided I would take the bus from downtown Calgary to get home. There was a good service that dropped me off within walking distance, and I could then return in the morning to pick up my car.

At 11.00 p.m., I boarded the bus, and there must have been a dozen or so other people on board. Naturally I had a couple of seats to myself. As usual, it was a cold night, and the bus driver had the heat cranked up to its high-est setting to keep himself from getting too cold each time the doors were opened. At the back of the bus it was toasty warm. I defy anyone slightly inebriated and on a very warm, rocking bus to not to fall asleep. I was sound asleep in no time. The bus went from downtown to the end of the run in Southeast Calgary. I was still asleep. The driver had a philosophy of "let sleeping dogs lie."

Around 1.00 a.m., I was back downtown, and the driver had to wake me up as it was the end of the line. Naturally I woke with a start, not knowing where I was. I had been asleep for two hours and found myself almost at the exact same spot. Obviously I was a little upset with the driver, but he had seen it all before and was unconcerned.

With the service shut down for the evening, I had the choice of ordering a taxi or driving home. I felt that after two hours of sleep I had sobered up enough to drive home, and besides, I didn't have the money for a 20 minute cab ride.

I hopped into my bright green Porsche, not the best car to be driving in this situation, and headed south on Macleod Trail. As with most roads in Alberta, it is almost straight, but there is one point where the road curves around a small hill. I was happily motoring along, and as I rounded the curve, there in the distance, was a bunch of flashing lights. My heart sank. I had heard that the Royal Canadian Mounted Police (RCMP) set up random checkpoints, but I had never seen one. My first instinct was to turn around, but I realised that at this point the road was one way, the northbound lanes separated by the hill from the southbound ones. The checkpoint had been chosen very strategically. There was no way out.

"Good evening, sir. Where are you coming from, and where are you going?"

"I have come from downtown, and I am going home." I had learned from many past experiences not to play around with people in authority.

"Have you been drinking sir?"

"Yes, I have had a couple of scotches," I continued, feeling like a criminal. I had spoken truthfully, although I didn't let on how many a couple really was. I knew he could smell whiskey on my breath, even though it was well over two hours since I had my last drink.

"Please pull over there," the RCMP ordered, pointing to a line of three cars being attended to by three other policemen. There was another cop waiting for me! The rush of adrenaline seemed to alert all of my senses quicker than any time before.

I pulled over to my appointed executioner who immediately asked for my drivers' license, insurance, and registration documents.

The insurance was the easy part, and was the first piece of paper he reviewed since it looked familiar to him. The insurance papers went to the bottom of the pile, and the next item was the registration. He had seen nothing like it. Neither had I for that matter.

"Is this your registration sir?" he queried with a frown.

"Yes," I replied in as clear a voice as I could muster. But feeling that my answer was inadequate I continued, "I recently imported the car from Germany and have not yet obtained the Alberta registration papers."

The bewildered cop must have stared at the papers under his flashlight for about 15 seconds — seemed like 15 minutes to me — and then moved the document to the bottom of the pile before turning his attention to my drivers' license.

Alberta drivers' licenses, like all licenses today, did not look like the English driver's license I gave to him, which in those days was just a sheet of paper, no photo. He inspected it with some intensity. It was 1977, and the license expired in 2011. He turned it over several times, not knowing what to make of it.

I could almost hear his thoughts. This driver has Canadian insurance papers, German registration, and an English driver's license. If I take this case any further I will be sorting out paperwork all night. He gave the papers one more shuffle and announced, "You are free to go — please drive carefully."

With a heartfelt "thank you," I drove home very carefully as instructed.

Suzan was really concerned about what could have happened to me and was waiting up.

"Oh God, what an evening," I moaned as I walked into the house, a little surprised to see her.

"I don't mind you going out for an evening of fun with your colleagues," Suzan retorted somewhat annoyed, "but don't come home moaning about it."

She had a point I suppose.

We tried to go to the Rockies as much as possible. There was so much to see and do there. Coming from England, the wildlife was like nothing we had ever seen before. Every trip in the summer months we would see black bears, grizzly bears, deer, elk and, less frequently, moose and mountain sheep. For the most part, the wildlife was fearful of humans, and there was no need to worry about their presence. When walking in the backcountry we always made a noise to alert any animals that we were there. Having Suzan with us was always a benefit: she was scared — or should I say more alert than most of us — and would be constantly looking in every direction as we walked along, and she was always talking so much that nobody else had to do a thing about making any sort of noise.

Barbecuing out in the wilderness was always fun — we usually took some ribs or steaks with us on our trips. The Canadian parks have plenty of barbecues available, and we became very proficient at making wonderful lunches. The only problem was that the tantalizing smell of the barbecuing meat would waft across the forest and alert the bears in the area. Often you could see one or two of them through the trees looking at you, but we never had any trouble. Suzan, rightly so, always kept the car door open so that she could scoop up the children into the car in case of an emergency. I always felt that poor Basil the bloodhound would get it first in the unlikely event they decided to attack.

There was one campground, Rampart Creek Campground, that had a particularly bad problem with black bears. One instance stands out. We were with my mother and her companion, introducing them to the wonders of outdoor cooking and the wildlife in the area when Suzan spotted several black bears through the trees. There were signs at the entrance of the campground warning visitors that there were many bears in the area, which naturally put Suzan on high alert. When they started to circle us, Suzan decided that it was time for us to retreat, so the half-cooked ribs, along with two children, four adults, and the dog were hurriedly loaded into the car.

The bears were a menace in that area. Even though the park rangers thought they had come up with bear-proof trash containers, the bears still managed to get in. It was a very amusing sight to see them scramble into the container and then every so often see them poke their head out to see what was going on. My mother thought it would make a great photograph, so she approached the container. She managed to place herself next to a ranger's truck with the bin on the other side, giving her a sense of security. As she was setting herself up for the picture, (it's amazing how long that can take), the ranger jumped into his truck and drove off revealing a sleeping black bear only a few feet away!

Life couldn't have been much better. I had a good job, a nice home, and new friends — a whole new life. And even though we had loads of fun exploring the mountains in the summer and skiing in the winter, there were times when I felt things were not right. I felt low and lacked energy. I tried to convince myself that this was just some type of homesickness, but I wasn't really angling after anything in particular back in England

and recalled many times when I had similar feelings in England. I always seemed to come around from these emotions within a few days. Unfortunately, I took my feelings of frustration and depression out on the people I loved most.

Five children, five ponies, with me second from the left on Gypsy

My Dad and Mum in the mid-'50s

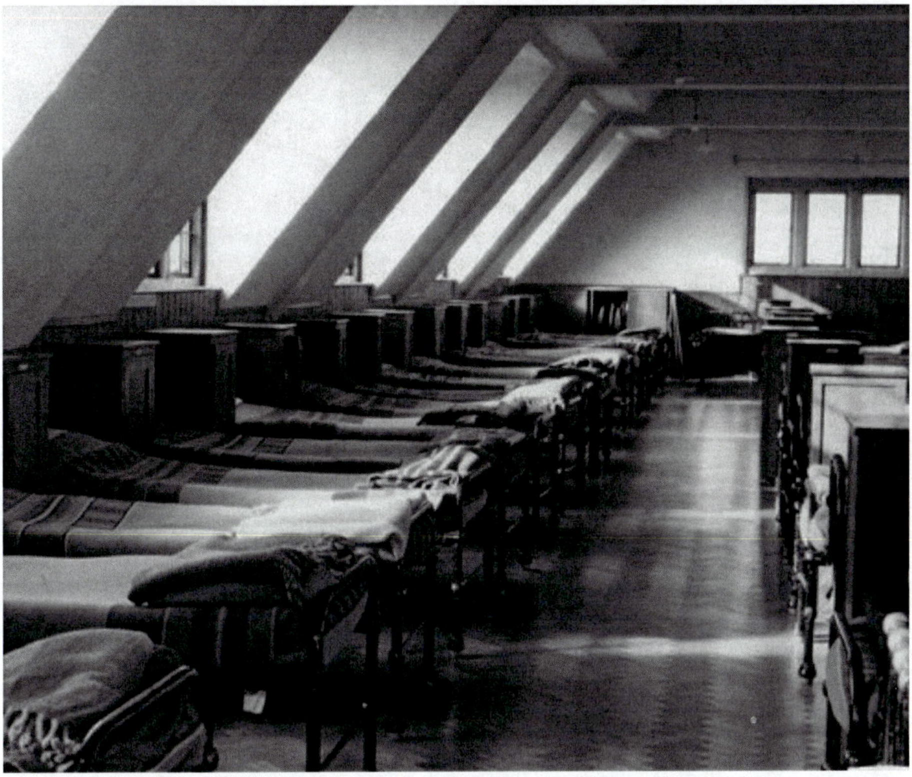

"New Dorm" at Ellesmere College

My official Trizec photo

New Years 2002 (showing signs of my weight gain)

Suzan with her dog, Mandy

At Aveda's salon prior to the operation

My daughter, Deb; granddaughter, Julia; and Craig

My son, Jeremy, and his girlfriend, Megan

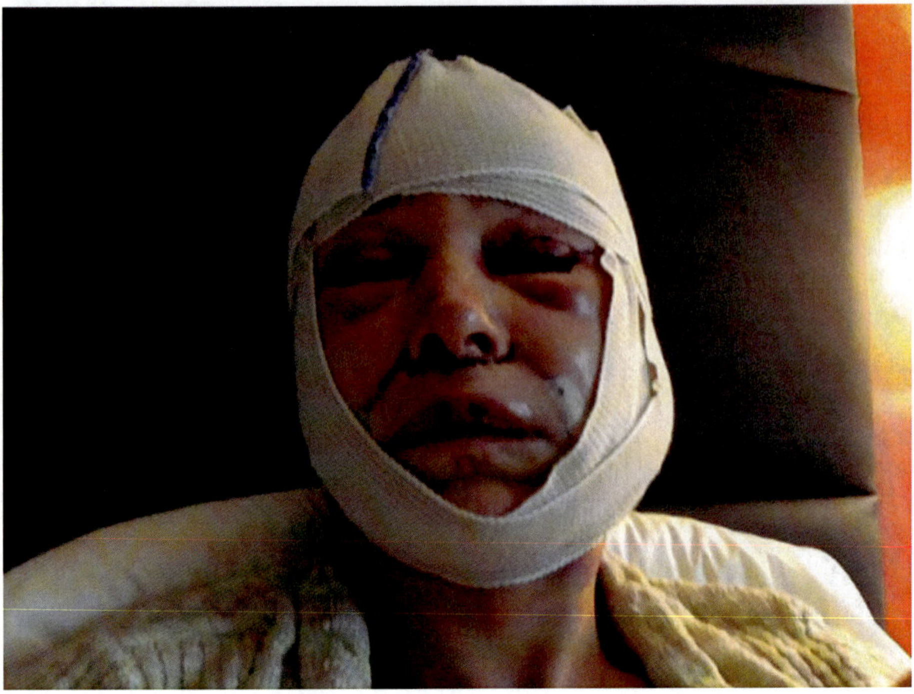

One day after Facial Feminization Surgery (FFS)

David Howell and me in Hua Hin, Thailand

Having a good laugh with David after a 45-year interlude

PART 5
DETROIT

CHAPTER 23

U.S.A.

One day I was asked to go to Tom Stephenson's office, the division's vice president. Glen was there, and I was a little concerned until they both smiled and asked me to sit down. Tom explained that the controller in Detroit had decided to leave the company, and the position was being offered to me. They would fly Suzan and me to Detroit where I could meet my potential new boss, Jack Berke, and check out the office and the area. It came as a great surprise, and I was flattered and excited about the opportunity. Glen wasn't too excited about the situation; not because he might lose me, but because he felt we were settling well in Calgary and would have a better life there. Neither Suzan nor I, at the time, were aware that Detroit had the distinction of being the "murder capital of the United States." The city had a huge problem with crime in general, and many families fled to the suburbs after the race riots of 1967, 12 years previously. While the Detroit suburbs thrived, the city itself went into a steep decline — a plight that still persists today.

Suzan and I flew to Windsor, Ontario, a small city situated on the other side of the Detroit River.

The airport was very small, so our luggage arrived quickly. Jack Berke was to meet us off the plane and take us to our hotel. A quick check around the arrival area, and it appeared that there was no one waiting to meet anyone. The time was about 7 p.m., and after about 15 minutes I was beginning to grow concerned. I only had his office number, and he didn't answer when I called. I didn't know what we should do. After 30 minutes there was only airport staff in the building other than us. Then, after another half hour, a car drove up to the building and two men emerged.

"Are you Peter Bamford?" one of them asked.

"Yes," I said politely. What I wanted to say, "Yes, and where the hell have you been! My wife and I have been stranded here in a strange place! How damn inconsiderate of you."

"Hi, my name is Jack." Introductions were made, no apologies or explanations were given and off we went.

The next day we met at Jack's office. He had arranged for a real estate agent to take Suzan around the northern suburbs to look at houses while Jack and I spent some time going over the controller's position — I think I understood the position better than he did. We then went on a tour of the buildings he was responsible for. There was also a building in Atlanta and a shopping mall in Clearwater, Florida that needed to be accounted for. Everything seemed to be straightforward, and I was strongly leaning towards accepting the position. But first I had to check with Suzan to see how she felt.

Her reaction was the complete opposite of mine. She had come back from her real estate tour very disheartened. The houses she had seen were expensive compared to Calgary, and there weren't any that she liked. She had arranged for us would look at houses together the next day. We were on our way to look at the first house on the agenda when we passed a new development that had two show homes visible from the road. One was quite "English" looking with false beams on the exterior.

"I love that one!" exclaimed Suzan.

"Oh, we can take a look at that," Mary, our realtor said. "It is in the Troy area, and they have good schools. And the builder has a good reputation."

Suzan and I loved it! Better still, there was one available on the private 5-acre park within the development. In the park, there was a private tennis court and an old gazebo, and I could envision the children playing in the area quite safely. As always seems to happen, it was the last one available on the park, and we needed to move now if we were going to buy it. Our offer was accepted, and we had a home in Troy, Michigan, a suburb of Detroit! I never did get to see the first house we were heading to.

We went back to Calgary and stunned our friends by announcing that not only had I accepted the job offer in Detroit, but we had already bought a house!

Our move to the United States was reasonably straightforward, other than the U.S. trucker's strike, which delayed our furniture and other belongings by three weeks. Although frustrating, it was not a problem. In any case our house was not entirely ready, but we were able to make do with what we brought ourselves. I had no problem crossing the border with a shotgun that my brother John had given me, but the custom officials were very focused on the wine and spirits I was bringing with me. I can't imagine what their problem was; I think they thought I was a dealer! It seemed to me that they had their priorities backwards.

I started to sort out what I found to be a poorly managed, overstaffed accounting department. The office was also very outdated with a telephone system where the operator had jacks and cables to plug in to connect the various parties. The computer system was archaic and ready for the Henry Ford Museum. There were two huge safes that were locked every night, but

I never did understand why. And then there was the ladies lounge where they could take a rest if they were feeling whatever they feel at certain times of the month. It seemed to me that the smokers used it most often. We had none of this in the Calgary accounting department, and I planned to model the Detroit office after Glen's accounting department.

There was another surprise in store for me: in the corner of my new office there was a pile of papers about two feet high. I asked the departing controller what they were, and he calmly announced that they were tax forms and other various returns that he hadn't had time to deal with!

"You have got to be kidding," I uttered in shock. "I have absolutely no knowledge of U.S. tax returns or any other returns for that matter."

"Well you are the controller now — it's no longer my problem." He continued, "If you need to get hold of me, here is my number in Chicago. You will find Peggy, your new secretary, very helpful. Good luck!" then he left. Wow, two feet of returns to file, I wasn't expecting this.

I decided to meet with the staff individually to find out who they were, what they did, and give them a brief outline of what I wanted to accomplish at the company.

The first person was Joan, the accounts payable clerk. We had a nice chat; I explained that I planned to upgrade all the equipment; alter the layout and décor of the office, which was awful; and increase camaraderie, which the ex-controller had said was not good. Obviously I didn't want to get into the staffing levels. I later heard that when she left my office, everyone was anxious to know what happened and what was discussed.

"Well he's really lovely," she declared, "but I didn't understand a word he said!"

The staff was diverse. Peggy was as efficient as my predecessor claimed and very loyal to me. The rest of the staff despised her and her cunning ways.

Scott, my assistant controller, was hardworking, but he made stupid mistakes. One time he made a mistake on a quarterly report that was submitted to corporate. It had been a bad day, and this was the last straw. I bumped into him in the hallway, where I berated him for the mistake. Later that day he came to my office and said he didn't mind being told off for his errors but that it wasn't right for me to do it in front of the other staff.

"Scott," I said, "you are absolutely correct. Please accept my sincere apologies, it won't happen again." And it hasn't, to him or anyone else for that matter.

One day he came to my office and asked if he could have two weeks medical leave.

"Well, of course," I said expressing concern, "what's the problem?"

"Oh, I have to go in for chemotherapy."

"That's terrible," I said in shock, not knowing exactly what chemotherapy was at that time but knowing enough to know that it wasn't good.

"Just give me a doctor's certificate and everything will be in order."

Scott called me from the hospital several times to let me know how things were going and said he was going to have to be there a week longer.

"Whatever it takes." I assured him. It wasn't until a few months later, after he had left the company that Peggy told me he wasn't having chemotherapy but was in a drug rehabilitation program. Now I was starting to wonder whether other members of my staff had a drug problem. There were a few candidates.

As controller I had control over many things, including treasury and banking responsibilities for the Eastern U.S. division. The Detroit Bank and

Trust had a large branch located in the building, so it was prudent to keep our accounts there. The bank manager was extremely pleasant and helpful and bent over backwards to help me in any way he could. Opening new accounts, purchasing commercial paper, transferring money to Calgary; my requests were never a problem, and he sorted out all the paper work. Or so I thought. One day I had a call from the bank, the caller announcing that he was the new bank manager.

"What happened to Mr. White," I demanded, knowing quite well that banks were notorious for switching their managers around.

"He decided that it was time to retire," the new bank manager noted. "I was wondering if I could set up an appointment to meet with you in your office."

"Sure," I replied, and we set a time and date.

He was a lot younger that I expected, and he probably thought the same of me. After the normal pleasantries he started out by saying that my records with the bank were in total disarray, and I would have to get them in order quickly if the company was to remain a customer.

"Excuse me," I declared in an aloof and rather angry voice, "but your records are your concern, not mine. I am your customer and would be happy to take my account elsewhere if that's what you want. Mr. White never treated me like this, and I am not about to let you do it."

"Well Mr. Bamford, I'm sorry to say that Mr. White has left his customers with no paperwork completed, and I have been made bank manager of this branch to sort out this mess."

"Oh," I replied, feeling a little sorry for him since he was only trying to do his job. Even though he needed some lessons in diplomacy, I told him I would help him where I could. The next day I went to the branch where I spent about one and a half hours signing documents to straighten everything out. Pleased with his accomplishment, he asked me out for lunch. I felt that I was beginning to strike a bond with him, so we decided the next day was as good as any.

The new bank manager called me about 9 a.m. the next morning to cancel the lunch appointment.

"I'm sorry to hear that, is there a problem?"

"Well, yes," he continued, "I have a dead security guard lying over my desk in a pool of blood!" Apparently the bank's guard committed suicide during the night. "I really don't feel like lunch, and besides I have the Detroit police here asking me all sorts of questions."

"No problem," I announced sympathetically, "we can set another date. Seems that you are having a rough first week on the job here."

"Yup, it seems that way doesn't it," he said solemnly.

Most of my staff were pleasant people, some more competent than others. Those who were not up to par had to go, and obviously I tried to hire only qualified people. One such employee was Carl: he was well-qualified and presented himself appropriately in the interview. I hired him as the replacement assistant controller. Unfortunately, he had a mouth than ran like a motor; no, like a racing engine, and his comments were not always welcome or pleasant. He had an opinion about everybody and everything. Now I knew why he was on his second marriage. But I have to say in his favor, his work habits were good, as was his performance.

One of the more colorful personalities was a young girl, Dana, the computer operator. She was extremely moody but was good at her job — the reason she stayed on. Peggy had taken a suspicious liking to her and was always defending her. As time progressed the situation deteriorated. After a meeting out of the office, I came back to find the department in turmoil.

What the heck's going on?" I demanded.

"Dana broke into Jack's liquor cabinet and has helped herself," someone stuttered. "Now she's on a rampage."

"Don't be ridiculous, she would never do that!" I remarked calmly.

I had hardly finished my words when the main door to the office flung open and in stormed Dana. She brushed passed me and ran down the corridor.

"Dana, come back here at once," I demanded. She didn't come. So I took off to find out where she had gone. Someone pointed to an open cabinet and to my utter astonishment, there she was, curled up like a little girl perched on top of a stack of computer printouts.

"Please take Dana home," I asked Peggy, knowing that she knew where she lived. Naturally, Dana lost her job.

Jack left Trizec nine months after I arrived and was replaced by a young leasing manager from Los Angeles. I don't know why he was given the position because he knew absolutely nothing about management and only a little more about leasing. He was cocky and loud-mouthed, and his Californian lifestyle just didn't fit in the Detroit office. He lasted just over a year when another new manager was appointed.

I had known Brent from my time in Canada — he was the property manager for our Vancouver properties — and liked him. He had been promoted to the LA office and came to Detroit as a vice president. Brent was a superior manager and made many positive changes in the Detroit office. He was very supportive of the controllers department and moved our offices into a greatly upgraded space and hired a new leasing manager, Mike. He also did much to improve morale within the office.

Brent implemented softball games, improved Christmas parties, and started summer picnics for all the Trizec employees. At one summer picnic we had reserved a picnic site at the Metro Beach Park on Lake St. Claire. These sites were ideal for company picnics, as they provided cooking areas as well as a large grass expanse for games or relaxing. Unfortunately, when we arrived we found that there had been a mix up in the reservations, and there was no place for us to go. With 80-90 employees turning up at any moment we searched for a suitable area. The best we could do was a grassy area next to a waterway that was connected to Lake St. Claire. I think it was a boat trailer park, but there were very few trailers. Under the circumstances, it was suitable.

We were all enjoying ourselves when we heard a noisy rumbling sound that became louder and louder as it got closer. It was obviously a large boat with a couple of V8 engines. Everyone was intrigued to see what boat it was, so all eyes were on the waterway. First a long point appeared, which then transformed into the sleek shape of a racing hull. On the hull, in bold letters was the name of a restaurant in the Fisher Building, who was always delinquent on their rent. Now we knew why! And finally the driver and passengers appeared. The driver, the restaurant owner, looked very embarrassed when he saw and recognized us. But he was not nearly as embarrassed as Carl's wife who was sunning herself on the back of this very expensive boat in her bikini! This was one time when the wind was taken out of Carl's sails. They divorced soon after, and Carl was headed for his third marriage.

CHAPTER 24

SHEBA

We were on our way to being established in our new neighborhood of Strawberry Hill. Many families that occupied the 50 homes of the subdivision were similar in age and standing in life. But it was not this fact that made the neighborhood special. Almost everyone got along with each other and became involved in the many activities that were organized. It never struck me as unusual that we had summer picnics in our private park with bike parades for the kids, tennis competitions, progressive dinner parties, golf outings, etc. It was only later that I found out that other neighborhoods didn't do this and that we had stumbled into something special.

Everything was going well, but our family seemed incomplete. We didn't have a dog. Basil had died in Canada, 18 months previously, and the children were at an age where they would benefit from one. As one of their Christmas presents that year, we promised the children a dog.

We knew of a "leader dog for the blind" school in nearby Rochester, MI, run by the Lions Club, who did fantastic work in this field. Apparently it is one of the leading schools of its type in the country. We also discovered that you could put your name down to take dogs that failed to meet their high standards. Suzan and I both had visions of a well-trained Labrador or a German Shepherd who had failed in the last stages of the training. We called the school and found out that there was a two-year waiting list! Our hearts sank, but we put our names on the list anyway. We were somewhat shocked and told our friends of the story. Then we heard that a friend of a friend was at the top of the list, and now they didn't want a dog. Apparently we could substitute our name for theirs, which we did. About two weeks later we got a call from the school saying that they had a 7-year-old Labrador available from a man who had passed away. Suzan rightly thought that it was not fair on the kids to have a dog that old and asked if they had a younger dog available.

"Well, we have a 2-year-old female, a Labrador/German Shepherd mix, that hasn't been through the full program," was the reply.

We thought that there would be nothing to lose by taking a look, so we piled the very excited kids into the station wagon, not knowing what to expect.

A white-coated man met us with the dog. He arrived with a very skinny, frightened, and trembling dog; brown in color and fairly large in size. The dog was shaking so much you could almost hear her bones rattle. We didn't know what to think.

"What sort of dog is it?" we inquired.

"She's a Labrador/Shepherd mix."

"Is she house-trained?" Suzan asked.

"We don't know."

"Is she good with children?" Suzan demanded.

"We don't know."

"What's wrong with her?" I said getting concerned by the white-coated man's short answers and lack of concern about placing the dog in a good home.

"It's on her report card. She has had all her shots, do you want her or not?" he said impatiently.

"Can we bring her back if she doesn't work out?"

"No, once you sign the paper the dog is yours."

"Can I see the report card?" I requested, running out of questions to ask.

"Here," he said handing me a sheet of paper, "if you want her just sign here and here."

At the top of the report it said the dog's name was Sheba. Such a sophisticated name for such an unsophisticated dog. At the bottom of the sheet it said that the dog failed the course after two weeks because she was flighty, immature, and irresponsible. Ummm, I thought slowly, she will fit right in.

"Well, what do you think Suzan?" I said, knowing that realistically she would be the one to take care of her.

"Oh *please*, Mom!" both the children said excitedly having only seen one dog.

"Okay," Suzan said. I signed the papers, and we were now the owners of a wild dog.

The first week with Sheba was hell, and we seriously didn't think she would last with us very long, even though she was house-trained. She was everything the report card had indicated. But after a few weeks she settled down to become the most wonderful, well-traveled, spoiled pet, adored by the whole family and the children in the neighborhood. She participated in everything, whether it was acting as the police dog in the children's games, cross-country skiing, camping, hiking or joining in our normal family routine.

CHAPTER 25

BACK PROBLEMS?

Coming to United States through Canada was a blessing. Although I didn't realize it at the time, the culture of Canada is roughly halfway between that of England and the United States. So I was introduced to the differences gently. The U.S. attitude towards guns, drinking, education, TV programming and politics are all very different than that in England. Even the language is full of nuanced differences that often go unnoticed.

Soon after I took the controller's job in Detroit, a decision was made to build a large office building next to the Fisher Building where I worked. The contractor was Turner Construction, a large international contractor, who had offices in our building. I had the overall responsibility for the accounting on the project, and this brought me in close contact with Turner's controller, Mike. He was a true Bostonian with a strong but pleasant accent.

Mike's immediate family lived in Columbus, Ohio, and he would fly home every Friday night and return on Monday morning. His assistant controller, Larry, became a good friend of Mike's, and the three of us would often have lunch together. On Friday nights, we would normally go to the bar at the St. Regis hotel next to the construction site and have two or three beers. Larry would always then drive Mike to the airport. I don't know how he ever made his plane, as he always left at the last minute, quite literally. They would drive like hell, and Mike would run through the airport where he would meet the flight attendants, who were normally holding the plane for a couple of minutes just for him. Obviously this is pre-TSA and all the security checks that travelers now have to endure.

Mike eventually bought a house in the northern Detroit suburbs and moved his wife and five children there. This took a lot of pressure off his weekend traveling chore but somewhat cramped his weekday bachelor style. I liked Mike for his easygoing ways, his good humor, and happy-go-lucky attitude. He had a charming young black secretary who wore her hair in cornrow braids. One day I was in his office when he called out to her.

"Hey Ropes, come here, could you?" I was in shock, being extra-sensitive about the race issues in Detroit. She came in smiling.

"Hey Ropes, I don't think you have met Peter, have you?"

"No," she said, "nice to meet you."

"You don't let Mike call you Ropes, do you?" I said to her in disbelief as Mike sat there leaning back in his chair, smiling.

"Oh, I don't mind Mike saying it. He's a really nice boss," she remarked as she turned around and left the room.

On Easter Sunday, the phone rang and it was Larry.

"Peter, this is Larry," he said, his voice trembling.

"Oh, hi Larry, what's up?"

"Mike's dead," he spurted out.

"What!? Mike's dead?" I was stunned. "Are you sure?" I questioned, not knowing what else to say.

Larry's voice was really trembling now, so I knew he wasn't playing around.

"He was playing basketball with his kids when he had a massive heart attack and died before any medical attention arrived. It's terrible, Peter. He was only 40. He has 5 young kids."

"Oh, Larry this is awful! I just don't know what to say. Thanks for letting me know."

"Yes Peter, you are one of the first people I thought to call. I guess I will see you in the office tomorrow."

"Okay Larry, I'll see you tomorrow. Bye."

The next day I met with Larry and we commiserated about Mike. Everyone was in total shock. I was even more shocked when Larry told me that Mike had heart problems before. It seems he didn't pay any attention to the changes in his lifestyle that his doctors had suggested. The visitation and the funeral were conveniently on the same day.

There was a short service in the funeral home and then off to the cemetery where there was another short service. Seeing the young children, I couldn't help but think back to my own father's funeral and wondered what was going through their minds. After the funeral we all went back to the home of the area vice president of Turner Construction's. There we tried to have a good old-fashioned Irish wake, but I, for one, was not in the partying mood. Had it been someone else's funeral and had Mike been there, I am sure things would have been quite different.

After a couple of years in Detroit we had settled in well, making many friends, mostly in our neighborhood. My work was challenging, and I was enjoying it. Life at home was happy, with the kids enjoying their respective schools and friends. As is often the case, this period of contentment was about to change.

In the fall of 1983 Suzan began to complain about a pain in her right leg. Normally I would brush this off, but Suzan is not a complainer and has a high tolerance for pain. Several weeks went by and the pain was getting worse, and she was having trouble carrying out her voluntary work at school and the normal household chores. From my perspective this was clearly becoming a major problem. In November, I persuaded her to talk to a friend in the neighborhood, Chris, who was an orthopedic surgeon. He felt that it was probably a ruptured disc in her spine, which was aggravating a nerve that went to her right leg. He saw her in his surgery the next day and decided she should go to the hospital for a CAT scan, which didn't show anything unusual.

We managed to make it through Christmas, but it was obvious that something had to be done. By January, Suzan couldn't move without excruciating pain, and Chris had her admitted to a small hospital in northern Troy. There he put her in traction, which should have alleviated the pain. It didn't.

In the meantime I had taken over the household. Get the kids up, give them breakfast, make Jeremy his lunch, see them off to their schools, make my bed — the kids can do their own — drive to work, carry out my job, go home early, give the kids a snack, prepare and eat dinner, visit the hospital for about an hour, wash up and do a quick clean on the house, put the kids to bed, collapse in a large chair with a couple of scotches, and then go to bed myself only to start it all over again early next morning.

I never realized until this point how much of an undertaking and responsibility a working mom has to endure. I tip my hat to all of you. I knew I couldn't keep this pace up for very long, but I needn't have worried. Our neighborhood friends jumped into action. They formed a roster to bring us dinner. They never failed. Always on time, always delicious. That is what true friendships are all about.

While Suzan was in the hospital it was extremely cold and windy. The walk from my car to the hospital door was an endurance test on its own, but it was always good to see Suzan, even if she was still in pain. Of course the kids were always very excited to see their mother. On their first visit, Debbie went rushing in and jump on the bed to say a well-meaning hello. Suzan grimaced. Debbie felt bad, Suzan even more so.

Dr. Chris and his colleagues decided that Suzan needed a lumber puncture to draw fluid out of her spine for tests. This procedure apparently went wrong, as they drew blood instead of the fluid that they had hoped for. I will spare you all the intricate details which patients and their families invariably give. It always amazes me how quickly everyone becomes an instant medical expert, knowing all the technical terms and procedures.

I went to visit Dr. Chris at his home where he told me that things didn't look good. He told me the reason they drew blood instead of spinal fluid was because they had punctured a tumor. She needed to be transferred to the Harper Grace Hospital in Detroit for more tests to decide how best to deal with it. Suzan and I discussed the situation, and we decided that Suzan's parents should come over from Holland to look after the kids (and me).

After further tests, it was discovered that Suzan's tumor was in her spinal cord and needed to be removed before it grew any larger and paralyzed her. Now I was in a panic. I had to find the best neurosurgeon to carry out the operation. The neurosurgeon who had been performing the tests was Dr. Ho. I bluntly asked him, "Who is the very best surgeon to carry out this kind of operation?"

"Well," he said with a look of honesty, "I believe that the very best surgeon would be Dr. So-and-so in Geneva, Switzerland." Then he said with a smile, "I believe that the second best would be me."

He was a very pleasant man with thick fingers, and I wondered how he could perform such intricate work. I asked some doctor friends of mine to check out his claim, and the reports all came back that he was an excellent neurosurgeon, especially with spinal cord operations.

Dr. Ho — a brother of Don Ho, the Hawaiian singer — explained to Suzan and me the intricacies and dangers of the operation.

"I have to go into your spine and scrape away the tumor from each spinal nerve making up the spinal cord. It is almost impossible not to cut or damage one or two nerves, but normally these tend to be minor nerves that you won't even notice. However there is always the possibility that I could sever or damage an important nerve that might cut the feeling in some part of the body below the waist or, in the worst case, could leave you paralyzed. We don't think the tumor is malignant, but it is imperative that it be removed. Do you have any questions?" There were plenty of questions I could have asked, but I could not bring them to mind.

"Yes, how long will the operation take?" Suzan asked.

"All being well, about six to seven hours." Then after a pause he continued, "If that's all, you'll probably want to talk things over," and he left the room.

I sat there stunned.

"How do you feel?" I asked Suzan, not knowing what else to say.

"Oh, don't worry — they have told me all of this before. I have it all planned out if I become paralyzed." She then went into some detail how she was going to manage everything, even her garden. I just sat there in amazement.

The day of her operation arrived quickly, and I was at the hospital early to give her some encouragement. She could hardly walk and was in extreme pain. I settled down for a long day in the waiting room put aside for spouses and close friends of those having operations. I knew I was in for the long haul, so I had brought tons of work from the office. While others flipped their way through magazines or paced the floor, I was busy writing notes, reading correspondence, dictating letters and memos, signing checks, etc. I am sure the others thought I was a very callous person, but as far as I was concerned, Suzan was in Dr. Ho's hands, and there was no point worrying about her operation at this point.

After six hours, I ran out of work. I had word that she was still in the operating room, and it would be some time before the operation would be over. Then about seven hours after the operation had started, I was called to see Dr. Ho. I was obviously concerned and when I saw his face, I was even more concerned. He wasn't smiling and looked terrible, tired, even exhausted. He told me that he had completed his work and the rest of the team was finishing up. She had done very well, and he thought only two nerves were damaged. He wouldn't know how this would affect her until she was fully alert. I was very relieved at the good news, even if it was conditional.

After eight hours in surgery and recovery, she was alert and all the tests were performed immediately. Thankfully, they found all parts of her body were functioning normally and now, so long as she did her prepared routine of exercises every day, she could do everything she was doing before the operation.

CHAPTER 26

ATLANTA

I n 1982, my career was proceeding as planned. The accounting department was streamlined and performing well. All reports and corporate filings for the many subsidiaries were completed accurately and in a timely fashion, and the accounts receivable had been greatly reduced. But my real interest was not in "bean counting" but in property development and management. I advised my boss Brent and he said he would think about it. It was about that time that Brent was promoted to be a senior vice president in the corporate office and recommended Mike, the Leasing Manager, to be the Divisional Manager and me to be the Director of Operation. Personally, I thought it should have been the other way around, as did many other people. However, I was now out of the accounting field and into operations, which was terrific.

Trizec was booming, acquiring major holdings in the Hahn and Rouse companies, two well-known retail developers. We were developing first-class office buildings all across North America. I was well thought of and became a vice president in 1986. November of that year was fast approaching, which meant my 40th birthday was about to be celebrated. Celebrated by all, except me. The occasion sent me into a tailspin and a deep mental slump. My depressions hit me hard, and I took to taking off in my car, going for long drives. I set out not knowing where I was going, how long I would be gone, or what I was going to do. Poor Suzan was left at home worried sick. Suicide crossed my mind many times on these drives, but thankfully I never tried.

My business trips were frequent, and I almost always carried two bags, one bag with my business attire and the other with my female garb. I had now built up a small wardrobe from which I could select. Building up a wardrobe was no easy matter. Obviously, I couldn't try the clothes on in the store, but I became quite proficient at choosing the correct size by holding the garment up in the air. As a male wandering around the female clothing sections of a store department store or in a women's clothing store, choosing clothes was somewhat embarrassing, especially if I had to stand in line to pay. But I had an "I don't give a damn" attitude, and other than getting the occasional judgmental stare, nobody ever said anything. Of course, it was so much easier if I had Suzan or a female friend with me. One such friend was Marge, a manager who worked for me in Atlanta. I confided in her about my double life, and she was so accepting and supportive. We used to go out shopping and afterwards we would have dinner together in my room. Just two girls having a fun evening.

A hotel room was the perfect place to let my female side come to life. Sometimes I would venture out into the night, with darkness being my friend. Expressing my female side was important to me and kept me somewhat sane. I dressed up whenever possible. In England I would roam around my five acres of garden and fields at Upper Birch when I was alone. It was very private there. I felt free.

On my trips to Atlanta, I would normally stay at the Ritz-Carlton. Besides being the nicest hotel downtown, it was also the closest to my office. On one occasion I decided to go outside, but not wanting to walk through the lobby, I decided to go down the back stairs that were to be used in case of a fire or another emergency. Everything was fine until I opened the door to the street. I stopped dead in my tracks as the door shrieked in the loudest squeal you could imagine! That threw my heart up somewhere around my throat and instantaneously I decided on a hasty retreat. I swung around to start my climb up the 10 floors of stairs I had just descended, only to see a security camera pointing right at me.

Great! I thought sarcastically.

I nonchalantly strutted passed the camera and then ran up six flights of stairs (three floors) where I tested the door to see if I could get back in. Often in office buildings, once you are in the stairwell the only way out is through the exit door at ground level. (In an emergency situation, like a fire, the doors automatically unlock.) Fortunately, this wasn't the case at the Ritz-Carlton, but I decided against taking the elevator, feeling very unlady-like after my three-floor dash. So I slogged my way up the remaining seven floors and reached my room without incident, physically and mentally exhausted.

Highs of one night could lead to lows the next day, and on one of these days I had scheduled a meeting in our conference room on the 23rd floor for 10 a.m. 10 a.m. came and went, and no one was there. 10:05, 10:10, 10:15 passed and still no one had arrived which absolutely infuriates me as a manager. The whole point of having a set time to meet is to minimize down time for everyone and maximize efficiency. Since it was an internal meeting I was sure they all had good excuses, which they did. But I let them know that I wasn't happy starting the meeting 15 minutes late and that in the future I expected all meetings to start on time, and if there was a problem, they were to call me personally and let me know.

While I was waiting, I stood close to the floor to ceiling window looking down the 23 floors to the street below. My mind wandered and within five minutes I had scratched out a verse.

230 Peachtree

Oh window, window up so high,
A welcome sight should you wish to die.
Stand there quivering, then let go,
Leaning forward ever so slow.
There's no way back, she begins to fly

Down to earth to end this lie.
There are no screams, there is no pain.
Oh! Not to worry, the man's insane.

I quickly refocused as some staff started to wander in and eventually got the meeting underway.

My drinking had increased, and my trips away from home didn't help this problem. Feeling lonely, I would often hang out at the hotel bar and strike up conversations with the barman or other guests sitting at the bar. One night while staying at the Ritz-Carlton, I felt too low to sit at the bar and chat, so I decided to be a loner at a table. I was drinking liquid gold as David Niven, the actor, once so aptly described Scotch, and with no one to talk to, I started to scratch out a verse on a napkin.

The Ritz

I feel like screaming!
"What is the meaning?"
I feel like shouting
in mental outrage.
I was born a man
it was not the plan.
Now what do I do
to live life through.
You think I'm male
but I'm set to fail.
As from the start
t' was in my heart
to live my life,
and face the strife,
as a female.
What a tale!

CHAPTER 27

UNIONS

I really enjoyed my new position at Trizec as Director of Operations. There were numerous things to learn, and I had several new ideas to implement. I had a great team of property managers who were, for the most part, happy to gain a different perspective on a well-trodden path.

The manager at the Atlanta property had been problematic, and I was interviewing several candidates in the office there. A panicked call came up from security at the lobby desk stating that people were demonstrating in our lobby. With no property manager, I stopped interviewing and went down to see what all the fuss was about. Sure enough, there were 20 to 30 people in our lobby holding signs and chanting. They represented the Service Employees International Union (SEIU) and were trying to unionize our cleaning and engineering staff. There was a young black man, tall and thin, leading the group. I was angry, as they were not only trespassing but were also disrupting the everyday workings of our building. There was no discussion. I told him in no uncertain terms to get out of my building immediately or I would call the police. I added that he had to get off my property entirely which included the plaza.

He immediately instructed his group to leave, which they did, presumably to go to the next building. Nothing came of their actions, and the buildings remained nonunion. In retrospect, I am convinced that the young black guy was none other than Barack Hussein Obama, the community organizer! Who would have thought that these actions were grooming him to become the President of the United States of America one day?

One of the more challenging parts of my job was to negotiate new wage and benefit packages with the SEIU and Teamster unions. The union demands were always enormous, which inevitably raised the hopes of their members. While it was always understood that our employees would receive a wage increase and perhaps additional benefits, it was never to the scale that the union demanded. Mostly, our differences could be sorted out and a contract signed for three years after some hard bargaining.

There was one such negotiation for the janitorial and engineering group at the First National Building, a large office building in downtown Detroit. The union (SEIU) demands were outrageous, and at that time we were trying to cut our already high running costs. Capital costs on this property were sky high, and the building was a cash drain on the company. While we were prepared to raise wages, the union and the company were miles apart. Threats of a strike began to surface, which made me uneasy, but we had to stand firm. Another building downtown had broken and given in to the union's demands, which was terrible for us, as it made us seem unreasonable. I made the decision to battle on. I checked with my corporate office in Calgary, and they gave me the backing I needed if the union struck us.

With neither side wanting to make a move, we reached an impasse. The state arbitrators were called in, as is required by law, to try reach a compromise, but to no avail. The scene was set for a strike. The union members gathered at the union hall and after, I am sure, a rousing speech by their representative, they voted to strike.

We had a plan worked out with a contractor to bring in non-union help, but in terms of total number of personnel, it was a far cry from our usual numbers. The staff and management of the building were commandeered wherever possible. One of our issues with the union was the lack of productivity. An average cleaner cleaned about 14,000 square feet a night while the industry standard was 30,000 square feet. Each of the new crew were given 30,000 square feet to clean, which was accomplished without too much difficulty. We proved our point, if only to ourselves. So by day, I was the Director of Operations; by night, I was a janitor pushing a vacuum and emptying waste bins.

The non-union help the contractor supplied was varied. At the start of one evening, I was walking about five of them to their respective areas to let them in and show them what to do. I was casually walking along the long marble hallways with a big bunch of keys, chatting away to a couple of the crew.

Out of the blue I heard a deep voice.

"Hey man, stop jangling them keys. They remind me of prison!"

"Oh yes, sorry," I replied in a very English way, as I hurriedly stuffed the oversized bunch into my pocket.

There were pickets outside the building every day, but other than the odd scuffle, they had no effect. The cleaning process for us could have carried on for months but after three weeks the union called off the strike. I felt sorry for the union members. They had given up a good part of their wages during this time frame and were made to picket during the cold winter days. The union funds had been depleted with nothing to show for it.

We gave them our final offer, which they accepted with a few minor face-saving changes. They all came back to work and now we had our work cut out to start rebuilding fences to once again gain their confidence and loyalty.

CHAPTER 28

SCHOOLING

Even though I didn't excel at school, I have always given my closest attention to my children's education. I wanted to make sure they had the best that I could afford without putting them through the ordeals that I faced. Their elementary education was at a public school within the Troy school district, which is considered to be one of the best in the Detroit Metropolitan area. Even though the middle and high schools in the area were good as well, I had heard of a private school very close to where we lived. George Booth, an Englishman who had made his fortune in the newspaper business of Detroit, founded Kingswood and Cranbrook, the girls and boys school, respectively. The grounds on which both schools are situated also housed an art academy and a science museum, as well as Mr. Booth's residence. The setting is beautiful, — very English looking with many of the buildings designed by famed architect Eliel Saarinen.

Other than the pure beauty of the school buildings and the grounds, the academics and extracurricular activities were very impressive. As private schools, the cost was not inexpensive and, of course, the children could go to the Troy schools for free. Fortunately, my mother had set up a trust for her grandchildren's education, which combined with my income from Lloyds, would help quite a bit. Suzan and I made the decision to send them to the Cranbrook/Kingswood schools even though it was a huge investment — thankfully one that was put to good use by both Debbie and Jeremy.

Neither was particularly keen on sports, so we didn't push them in any way to be involved. So often parents try to live their own sporting dreams through their kids, which can be disastrous for the child. The parent(s) then get so involved that they start arguing with other parents, and worse still, with the officials, destroying the whole purpose of kids participating in the first place. Jeremy tried many of the sports offered but really only enjoyed their ski program.

Debbie was very much involved with the modern dance program at Kingswood, which she loved. They had the opportunity to visit the USSR for a tour where they were well received. The highlight of the tour was their visit to Leningrad (now St. Petersburg, again), where they shared a program with the Kirov Ballet Company. The Soviets/Russians take their dance seriously, and it is not uncommon for students to share the stage with famous dance troupes.

Part of their tour took them to Tbilisi, Georgia in the south. It was at this time that the Georgians stated their declaration to break away from the USSR. The school kids witnessed the first protest march of the Georgian people against the communist government that eventually resulted in the downfall of the USSR. A week later, U.S. citizens were prevented from going there. Fortunately the children were out of the area before any serious fighting begun.

With excellent K-12 education behind them, they both went on to the university of their choice. Debbie went to Boston University (BU). The campus is spread out amongst the streets of Boston, which Debbie loved. She obtained her BA in English. Jeremy's first choice was the University of Colorado (CU) in Boulder. He applied to five universities, including BU, and was accepted by four of them. All but CU! This was a major disappointment to Jeremy, as he had set his heart on CU. He was now thinking about the University of Vermont in the lakeside town of Burlington. At that time I was attending a small meeting of BOMA (Building Owners and Managers Association) in Coral Gables, Florida and happened to sit next to the executive vice president of the association. I was telling him about Jeremy's unfortunate story.

"That's interesting," he said with a smile, "my brother has just taken a senior position assisting the President of CU. I will give you his address, and I suggest that Jeremy write him a letter explaining the situation. Feel free to mention my name." He made some suggestions as to how to word the letter and how to follow through if necessary.

Jeremy, of course, did exactly as he was told. It wasn't but three weeks later when Jeremy received a letter from CU apologizing for their error and that his application had somehow been misfiled. They had reviewed it again and were happy to offer him a place in their School of Business Management. It just goes to show how powerful networking can be.

CHAPTER 29

PERKS AND CELEBRITIES

One of the perks of being Director of Operations was that the contractors in many of our properties would often spoil you as a thank you for the business. This was perfectly legal so long as the value was reasonable, there was no financial gain, and it didn't affect the outcome of the next bidding process. I sometimes received tickets to concerts or sports games because the contractor also happened to have contracts with both the Palace, an outstanding facility built primarily for basketball and Pine Knob — now known as The DTE Energy Music Theatre — an outdoor amphitheater with covered seating in the front and lawn seating in the back. As a contractor they had access to some of the best seats in the house.

When Diana Ross played at Pine Knob, Suzan and I accepted the tickets to watch her solo performance. We had some of the best seats in the house, eight rows back, and center stage. About two-thirds the way through the show she decided to move off the stage into the audience. She moved gracefully down the aisle until she came to our row. She never stopped singing as she made her way past people's feet and stopped between Suzan and me. We sat there in utter amazement with our legs touching hers. To see her properly I had to cock my head completely back — all I saw were the fillings in her teeth. She felt comfortable enough to stay and sing two more songs in front of us before she moved back onto the stage. This was a truly remarkable moment for us to experience during a great concert.

I loved going to Pine Knob and Meadowbrook, a similar but smaller amphitheater that caters more to classical and jazz music. There is something magical about sitting outside, listening to a concert on a warm summer's night. When we first arrived in Detroit we decided to go and watch Neil Diamond at Pine Knob with two of our neighbors. We obtained lawn tickets and planned to take a picnic supper. This was going to be my first experience, and having heard much about Pine Knob, I was really looking forward to it. I was discussing the upcoming event with the marketing director at Trizec, and she told me that her daughter was employed there for the summer. She told me that if I wanted, her daughter could place some blankets on the lawn to reserve that space for us.

"That'd be great," I said, "but how will I know which blankets are ours?"

"Oh, you can't miss them, there will be a large red one and a large green one," she replied. I expressed my thanks and left her office.

On the day of the event we packed up our picnic, but we left a little late. As we walked into the park there was some muttering that we were unlikely to get a very good lawn position because of our tardiness.

"Don't worry," I said to the guys, "I have reserved a space for us."

"Oh no, Peter, you don't understand," one of them replied, knowing that it was my first time there, "you can't reserve lawn space. It's on a first come first serve basis."

"Well trust me, I'll find a decent spot for us."

"But Peter, the lawn will be a seething mass of people, especially at a Neil Diamond concert." The two began to laugh at my naiveté as the girls followed behind, just chatting away.

We entered the "auditorium," and sure enough there were masses of people on the lawn, spread all over the place especially center stage. The two guys, having ignored my previous comments, started looking frantically for a space. Just as had been promised, I spotted the two blankets laid out on the lawn with crowds of people all around them but not on them.

"Here's our space," I said pointing to the two blankets right in the center of the lawn.

The whole party now stared at me with a look of bewilderment. With their doubts beginning to slowly disappear, I ordered them to follow me. I led the way stepping over the crowds until I made the center of the blankets where I plonked myself down. The others who were holding back a little now started to move more briskly.

They gingerly sat down, with a feeling that they shouldn't be there and opened up the picnic baskets.

"Peter, how on earth did you manage to do this?" everyone asked me.

"I told you I had lawn seats reserved, but you wouldn't believe me, would you?"

"This is incredible. I have lived here all my life and have never even heard of this. And you have only been here just over a year and managed to reserve lawn seats at this year's most popular concert. Amazing," one of the guys lamented.

Tickets to Pine Knob were often available to us and they were always in the best seats in the front, which to me were not always the best seats, especially if a rock group was playing. The other tickets that seemed to be generally available were basketball seats at the Palace. The Detroit professional basketball team, the Pistons, played there, and back then they were one of the best teams in the NBA. Good tickets were hard to come by in general, but my source had the best: next to the team owner's seats, front row at the end of the court. Drink and snack waiter-service was available in this section and was put to good use. Being that close to the players gives one an appreciation of their size (6'8"–7') and agility.

The games were always exciting; each team normally finishing within a few points of each other. Once there was a game against the Atlanta Hawks. My usual seats were not available, but the secondary seats were just as good: front row, center court with nothing between you and the players. Unfortunately there was no beverage service available, so I had to slum it by obtaining my own. What a chore! The Pistons and the Hawks were a good match, and I was on the sweat flying line. These guys were both physical and aggressive. Even though there was plenty of space between the court line and the front row of spectators, the players often seemed awfully close. I was a little concerned but was somewhat comforted by the fact that the rest of the spectators appeared to be unperturbed and the players seemed to know what they were doing.

The game was going the Pistons way (again) when without warning a huge black shadow started to absorb my attention. I had no time to react. Maybe it was speed of the incident or maybe it was the beer, but I determined that I was about to be enveloped by a player. He was flying towards me at about 45°. The impact didn't really hurt, it was just the shock of having a very tall, very sweaty, Hawks player sprawled across my lap. Dominique Wilkins (6'8" and 230 lbs.) had just made contact with a disapproving Englishman. He mumbled an apology, I think, and as his huge, well-built body unwrapped itself from mine. I was going to say something but wisely decided not to.

Trizec's Eastern U.S. division was based in Detroit — Trizec's first acquisition in the United States was the First National Building in downtown Detroit. It wasn't soon after that the company purchased the Fisher Building and the Albert Kahn Building, about three miles north of downtown in the New Center Area. These buildings were situated across the boulevard from General Motors World Headquarters. The famous architect Albert Kahn designed all three buildings, and it was fondly known as Kahn's corner.

It was the seven Fisher brothers who commissioned Albert Kahn to design and build the Fisher Building. The Fisher brothers owned Fisher Body, a company in which General Motors purchased a 60 percent interest during the early part of the twentieth century. Presumably, this gave the brothers the wealth to commission Albert Kahn to design and build the building without a budget. The first stage was a 28-story tower with two eight-story wings off the tower forming an "L". The exterior of the building was granite for the first three floors and then white marble for the rest of the building except the back-of-house area. The interior had a cavernous three-level arcade with hand painted frescoes on the ceiling, which contained 60 percent gold leaf. The marble in the arcade was from every available mine at that time. Brass was the predominant metal used for door handles, elevator doors, air grills, etc. It is said that the amount of brass used when laid end to end would reach from Detroit to New York. The building originally had three levels of retail stores and a movie theatre, but eventually the movie theater became a theater for plays and musicals.

Everyone who came in touch with the building marveled at it, and those of us who worked there felt very fortunate. Trizec's divisional offices were located in the Fisher Building, and as a daily visitor I was constantly seeing something new. It might have been a saying written in gold leaf on the wall, a brass design on the elevator, or a marble sculpture on the exterior. As someone in the office building industry, I find the most astounding thing to be that the building from the first shovel going into the ground to the first tenant occupying the building took only 12 months. I still find it unbelievable, especially when one considers that it normally takes six months to build a cookie cutter-type house. Originally, the design for the building included a duplicate mirror image building on the other end of the block with a 50-plus story tower in the middle. The first stage of the building was completed in 1928 ,but unfortunately, that was the year of the stock market crash and the start of the Great Depression. Naturally, all other plans for further construction were scrapped. I loved the Fisher building and the numerous stories that went with it.

The huge Detroit Bank and Trust branch in the building (now known as Comerica Bank) decided to move to smaller premises on the first floor. The old bank space was leased to a Greek restaurant owner who carried out a spectacular job restoring the ceiling to its original glory and turning it into an excellent Greek restaurant. Often a group of us would visit the bar there and kick back after work. This normally happened on a Friday night and at first the bar was packed then the crowd normally thinned out as patrons left to make the trek north to Detroit's suburbs.

One night, Suzan and I went to the Fisher Theatre and decided to have a relaxing drink in Pegasus, the Greek restaurant, after the performance. We hooked up with a small group of Trizec employees who were left behind from the evening's social gathering. The bar and restaurant were quiet, and it made me think that they must make most of their money during the lunch hour and prior to the theater nights. Interestingly enough there was a live band playing jazz in the corner accompanied by a singer. We were preoccupied and didn't pay much attention to them. Without any warning there was a bit of a commotion at the entrance to the restaurant and all eyes focused that way.

None of us in the bar that night could have imagined what was about to happen. We couldn't believe our eyes. In walked Stevie Wonder with his entourage! His friends led him to the band where the singer excitedly announced what we had all just witnessed. Apparently, he had come to hear his close friend, the female singer, perform. She sang a couple more songs and then handed the microphone over to Stevie Wonder, who seemed more than willing to sing to the 30 or so of us in the restaurant and bar.

What a fabulous and unimaginable evening. It all seemed like a dream the next day. Naturally, we told our close friends in the neighborhood about it, but I don't think they really believed us. It was another one of those incredible events that Detroit kept producing for us.

PART 6
PERSONAL PROBLEMS

CHAPTER 30

DIAGNOSING DEPRESSION

All through my adult life I had spells when I just wanted to be left alone. It didn't matter what situation I was in or my whereabouts; I could be on a great vacation or at work. I'll always remember the time when we were on holiday with my sister Neenie and friends, skiing in Verbier, Switzerland. The skiing was at its best, and it was a beautiful, sunny day — I should have been in the greatest mood, but for some inexplicable reason I felt terrible and didn't want to have anything to do with anyone in our group. Of course that is sociably unacceptable, so I tried to mix in, which just makes matters worse. I felt down and lacked energy; sometimes things looked bleak, very bleak. I could only see issues in their worse perspective. I was angry, and I would hurt the people closest to me by saying or doing the most unreasonable things. Suzan and the children always put up with it, but then I suppose they had little choice. They knew eventually that I would pull out of it and become my normal energetic self again, but it was hard on them. These spells seemed to happen on a regular basis, normally in a four-to-five week cycle. Some of my mood swings were much worse than others. And although I never felt that things would change while I was in one of these moods, I would always come out of them in a few days. Then I felt fine, happy. Exuberant even. Life was a breeze, and I didn't seem to have a problem in the world. I could take anything that was dealt me. And so it went on.

It was a tiresome way to live, but that was the way I lived. I didn't know any better. I knew it was not normal, but I didn't really know what was wrong. When I was with people I didn't know or at work I would have to dig down deep not to show my emotions; when I was with my family I would not make the effort, which is probably why they took the brunt of my moods.

Suzan and I discussed the idea of my seeing a specialist. We asked a friend of ours — a nurse — if she knew of a reputable psychiatrist. She asked around and came up with the name of Dr. Jefferies. An appointment was made, and my first session seemed endless. Through all the questioning, he never asked anything that would lead me to tell him about my transsexualism. Towards the end of my time limit I said, "Dr. Jefferies, I think you should be aware that I believe that I am transsexual."

He mumbled something and scribbled on his notepad but offered no surprise, support, or sympathy. I needed at least some expression of feeling. It was soon after this that he advised me he was going to refer me to Dr. Jones, a psychologist in the practice. For some reason I felt slighted, probably because it seemed that he did not want to personally address my problems.

Dr. Jones did directly address my transsexual feelings, but only through hypnosis. He tried to dispel all notions of my femininity, but it had zero effect on me. I felt no differently than before. I was still depressed. As a psychologist, he was unable to prescribe medication, so that, combined with my lack of progress, led me to stop my sessions with him.

I started to suspect that when I mentioned my transsexualism to men that they somehow felt threatened by it. They had difficulty imagining how any heterosexual, masculine-looking male could possibly want to be a female. It was so outside their realm of logical thinking, and they didn't want to deal with it.

The saying "a problem shared is a problem halved" is so very true. At this point, I had relayed my problem to three people: Suzan, Dr. Jeffries, and

Dr. Jones. I felt very relieved after telling Suzan and somewhat better after divulging my problems to the professionals, but nothing really changed.

It was at this point that I decided to call John Hopkins University Hospital. Over the years, I had heard that they were the leading hospital for sex reassignment operations. I found their number and finally got through to someone who explained that the department had been closed down a few years back.

Closed down! Surely they should be expanding it and trying to figure out the multitude of feelings and different facets of the transgender community and, in particular, transsexuals.

Some days things seemed to be under control, but they really weren't. My moods were deepening, especially when I started to travel more. Maybe it was stress-related or maybe it was a normal progression of whatever was causing it. There were nights I would call Suzan from my hotel only to find myself crying for no apparent reason. I would cry myself to sleep. The next morning I would muster up all the energy I had to get me through the day.

At the office it was much harder to hide my moods. Mary, my secretary at Trizec, would often see me in this situation and would give a knowing look, a comforting look. She knew not to say anything other than "Shall I shut the door?" She knew I just wanted to be left alone.

I spent hours slumped in my chair staring at the blank wall behind me, completely immobilized. Nobody from my door could see that I was in my chair so that prevented them from disturbing me. At the end of the day I would drag myself to my car, drive home, and continue my lonely ordeal. I didn't want to talk or discuss anything with the family. Often, to be alone, I would go out for a drive in my car, not knowing where I was heading. Naturally this worried Suzan to death. The state I was in, she didn't know what to expect. I would be gone for a couple of hours but would always return home none the worse, or better for that matter.

At night I would have trouble going to sleep and would frequently find myself rolling around in bed, moaning with mental pain. It is a feeling that is hard to convey. Obviously something had to be done.

I called Dr. Jefferies again and made an appointment to see him. We had a discussion about my situation. I gave him all the details I could remember. He asked numerous questions, and I answered them all truthfully and sometimes tearfully.

"Have you ever been suicidal?" he asked out of the blue. The question took me by surprise.

"Yes," I replied, not knowing how else to say it.

"How would you have done it?"

"Probably by driving my car into a highway bridge." There were no questions as to 'why that way?' or 'what if you hadn't succeeded in your attempt?'

"On a scale of one to ten how close have you come to doing it?" he continued.

"Nine and a half," I replied truthfully and somewhat shamefully. And so the questions went on.

Dr. Jefferies prescribed me some medication.

"I am going to put you on Lithium, a well-tried drug to treat your manic-depressive illness and Prozac, a new anti-depressive drug." Obviously he had known since I had started talking what was wrong with me, but this was the first time I heard him say it: manic-depression. In many ways, it was a relief knowing that there was something wrong with me, something treatable.

"Okay," I said, "how long will I have to take them?"

"Oh!" Dr. Jefferies said surprised by the question, "This is something you will have to take the rest of your life. It will treat the symptoms but does not cure the problem."

"Oh no!" I replied genuinely shocked, "I have never been dependent on anything. I know it's going to help me, but I can't help feeling sort of disappointed in myself." I could tell by his look that Dr. Jefferies didn't understand.

Most drugs have side effects, and both Lithium and Prozac had many. Lithium listed, among others, drowsiness, tiredness, trembling of hands, weight gain, unsteady walking, diarrhea — all of which I experienced and, with the exception of trembling hands, continued the whole time I was on the drug. I felt like I was 90 years old, not a 38-year-old. I was unable to walk down the stairs without holding the handrail, I would trip over anything higher than half an inch, and I constantly had diarrhea.

Prozac had other side effects. They weren't as bad as Lithium, but I was constantly tired. Initially, I went back to Dr. Jefferies every week, then every month, and finally every quarter. I had my blood tested on a regular basis because of the affect the drugs can have on the liver. However, the drugs did their job in greatly reducing the depression and the side effects were worth enduring.

I was on these drugs for the next three years or so, and the side effects started to drain me. I put on a considerable amount of weight, going from 165 pounds to 222 pounds. My face looked bloated. I had constant diarrhea and never had any energy. In a discussion with Dr. Jefferies, he decided to take me off Lithium and replace it with Tegratol. This had to be carried out gradually.

However, no sooner had I started Tegratol, when one night I started to feel ill. I went to the bathroom until I felt a little better and returned to bed. I never made it. Just as in previous incidents of this type, I passed out, falling flat on my face — thankfully this time I fell on the carpet. Naturally, a startled Suzan flew out of bed to find me groaning on the floor in a cold sweat. Thank goodness Suzan had nursing experience while in England. Over the next couple of days I developed a red rash all over my body. I had swollen joints, tunnel vision, and hot and cold flashes. She and I determined that I was having a violent reaction to Tegratol, although Dr. Jefferies didn't seem to think that it was the drug causing these reactions. Nonetheless, he changed my prescription again, this time to Depakote, which treats the high and low swings of bipolar disorder.

The change to Depakote was wonderful. I felt like a new person. Many of the side effects of Lithium quickly faded while at the same time my depression stayed more or less under control.

It wasn't a "cure all." Sometimes I would have a relapse, but nothing of the magnitude I had previously experienced. I stayed with the Depakote and Prozac combination for several years. But one of the problems I still faced was a constant feeling of tiredness. I could have a good eight to nine hours of sleep and go to work feeling drowsy. On my way to work, I often had trouble keeping my eyes open. I can remember being within a quarter of a mile from my office feeling so tired that I pulled off the road into another office building parking lot. There I reclined my car seat and went to sleep! Often in the afternoons I was so sleepy that I would go to a city park in my car to sleep or in the winter to an open garage where I would sleep with my engine running to keep warm. This was not a good way to live.

After consulting with me, Dr. Jefferies ordered several more changes in my medication. I know that to most readers this section may seem to be a list of drugs with boring names and of little interest. This disease, while treatable, requires the right combination of drugs and that often can take a lot of trial and error. The right treatment will allow sufferers to function normally in society.

This disease is still not broadly accepted for what it is. It's not about strength and willpower of the individual — someone who suffers from clinical depression of any sort needs to know that there are plenty of us out there and that real help, not just advice, is readily available.

I also feel strongly that the more sufferers who go public, the more accepted this disease will become. It seems so strange to me, if not a little insensitive, that corporations and people in general turn their backs on depression sufferers who have gone public and taken the huge step of going to a psychiatrist to get the proper treatment and medication. That's a better alternative than having an employee who suffers from depression being a potential time-bomb running around without any professional help at all.

CHAPTER 31

LLOYD'S OF LONDON

Managing my career and ensuring that my family received the utmost attention combined with the conditions of depression and transsexualism to handle meant that my hands were full. However, another major problem was about to raise its ugly head; a financial one.

In 1976, I was chatting to a friend of James and Neenie's at a party of theirs about Lloyd's of London, the international insurance market. He was working at Lloyd's and told me something of its workings. I was interested in pursuing the possibility of becoming a member. To understand the major problems that Lloyds experienced in the late 1980s early 1990s, it is important to understand how this unique institution works.

Most people have heard of Lloyds of London, but few people understand how it works. Lloyd's[6], as it is now known, began in Edward Lloyd's Thames side coffeehouse in Tower Street in the City of London. Although the exact date of its establishment is not known, evidence exists that Lloyd's coffeehouse was well-known in London business circles by 1688. Edward Lloyd himself was not involved in the insurance business but provided the prem-

---

6. The facts regarding the History of Lloyd's were taken from the Lloyd's website - www. lloyds.com

ises with reliable shipping news and a variety of services to enable his clientele of ships' captains, merchants, and rich men to carry on their business of insuring ships and their cargoes. The wealthy individuals in the coffee house would each take a share of the risk, signing their names one beneath the other on the policy together, which is how they became known as 'underwriters'. Mr. Lloyd died in 1713, but the coffee house continued as a center for marine insurance.

As business thrived the underwriters became more organised. By the end of the 18th century the underwriters had elected a committee and moved to their own premises in the Royal Exchange, and only members were allowed to accept insurance business. The Society of Lloyd's was incorporated by an act of Parliament — the Lloyd's Act of 1871 — that provided the business with a sound legal basis and laid the foundations for today's market. Lloyd's is not a corporation in the normal sense with shareholders or a partnership, rather a group of people pledging their assets to cover losses in the insurance market and in return receiving the insurance premiums. Naturally, the members of Lloyd's, known as Names, hope that the premiums received will exceed any losses for that year. By the turn of the century, the traditional club of marine underwriters had become an international market for insurance risks of almost every type. Lloyd's became the preeminent insurance market in the world, especially when it came to shipping.

The institution of Lloyd's is steeped in history. Many of the traditions that were in place in the coffee house are still in place today. Syndicates work from 'boxes' — small work areas similar to a booth in a coffeehouse or restaurant. The working members of the syndicate sit at their boxes and the insurance brokers, representing their clients needing insurance, visit them to try to coax that particular syndicate to write a 'line'. Messengers in their red coats — called waiters, another allusion to the coffeehouse days — run errands and messages between the various boxes.

Each 'syndicate' is made up of many names and specialises in one type of insurance e.g. marine, aviation, motor vehicle, life, etc. A Managing Agent controls each syndicate, accepts risks on behalf of the whole syndicate, and is responsible for running all aspects of the syndicate. It is the Managing

Agent underwriter who decides which of the risks to accept and at what premium. It is he who negotiates the extent and conditions of coverage that the syndicate will assume. If the underwriter feels that the risk he accepted is too large he can reinsure with some other syndicate or insurance company.

Names have to pass a means test to show certain net worth. It is this net worth that determines the level that the name can underwrite, and it is the total of all names that determines the underwriting capacity of that syndicate.

The benefit of becoming a Name at Lloyd's is that all your money continues to work for you as it normally does in say the stock market and other than paying a few fees, there is no further investment in Lloyd's. Of course the downside is that you have to pledge all your assets in the event of a catastrophic loss. Furthermore, if one of the names in your syndicate is unable to pay his share then the rest of the names have to ante-up. This is unlimited liability at its finest!

After the party, one thing led to another and following a little soul searching, I decided that this would be good investment. Sure, I risked losing all of my assets down to the shirt on my back, but Lloyd's had been around for almost 300 years with an excellent record for the investors. Of course there had been some problems but nothing catastrophic. It seemed like a great investment to me.

I completed the endless paperwork and had numerous discussions with my Member's Agent before I finally visited Lloyd's for my personal interview with a few members of the Lloyd's Committee. The Lloyds building was impressive, the rooms imposing and elegant. The Lutine Bell hung in the center of the floor that, until recently, rang each time there was a ship lost at sea. The bell itself was recovered from a wreck that had been covered by Lloyd's. It was fascinating watching the brokers run from box to box getting the underwriter to sign a line. This was the institution I was to become a member of on January 1, 1977. I was to be in three syndicates that had been recommended to me by my agent. A Name has to place a great deal of trust in his agent.

Lloyd's works on a three-year accounting system — it takes that long for all the premiums to come in and claims to be paid off. Because of that, I unfortunately didn't expect any income from Lloyd's until the first part of 1980. The good news was that when I left Lloyd's, which I intended to do after the children's education had been paid for, I would receive income for three years after I resigned. There are some losses, known as long-tail losses, that aren't fully known even after three years, like asbestos and breast implant claims. So at the end of three years, in order to close the year in question, these claims have to be reinsured and will be covered by the Names in the syndicate where the loss is reinsured.

After my three-year wait, my annual cheque from my Members Agent arrived on a regular basis. Just as I expected, there were no surprises and the cheques, although not large, were certainly adequate.

In 1985 I had a call from my agent to inform me that Lloyd's was looking to greatly increase its capacity and suggested that I should join more syndicates. He pointed out that since I already was exposed to unlimited liability there was little to lose. So at his suggestion I joined 11 more syndicates for a total of 14. I could expect a nice bump in my income to occur in 1990. Because I was in the property management and development business, I was particularly close to the asbestos problem, which at that time was a huge issue. I told my agent not to put me in any syndicates underwriting insurance on asbestos or earthquake damage. Earthquakes and 'the big one' were constantly in the news in the United States around then.

The first sign of trouble was in 1989 when many syndicates were reporting losses. I wasn't too concerned, as several of my syndicates were showing good profits which counteracted any of my losses. However, 1990 and 1991 proved to be catastrophic years. Lloyds was hit by major claims from the Alpha oil rig disaster in the North Sea, Hurricane Andrew, the San Francisco earthquake, the Pan Am air disaster over Lockerbie, an oil rig disaster in the Gulf of Mexico, and to top it off, the asbestos claims were coming from all angles: property owners, school boards, individuals, etc.

There were several other major claims, and over the years of 1989 to 1992, the total losses amounted to approximately £14.7 billion or approximately $22 billion. Yes that is a billion with a 'B'. There was hardly a member that didn't get hit hard by these losses. Some Names, seeing no way out, took their own lives. A number declared bankruptcy. Many, especially those in the United States, formed action groups against their syndicates. I had lost all my investments but fortunately, Lloyds was not coming after my house, jewelry, cars, and other tangible assets.

I was obviously losing confidence in Lloyd's in 1991, but at that time didn't know how much insurance they had underwritten in the disasters that had occurred. I called my agent in the beginning of October 1991 and told him I wanted out. He was rather rude and curt, telling me that I should have done that in August. I didn't believe him, but the outcome was that I was a Name for 1992. I think he wanted me in so that he could continue to collect fees from me. It was then that I lost all faith in my agent. It seemed that some of my syndicates had been underwriting asbestos and earthquake losses contrary to my verbal orders to my agent. They were verbal orders, so there was nothing I could do. In retrospect, I don't think being in Lloyd's for 1992 made much of a difference. I was already wiped out. Of course the large increase in income that I had hoped for in 1990 didn't materialize, and my nest egg wasn't going to hatch.

CHAPTER 32

INSIGNIA

All good things come to an end, and this was certainly the case with my tenure at Trizec. The commercial real estate business tends to be a cyclical one, and at the end of the 1980s and the early 1990s the industry hit a down spiral. For Trizec, this was aggravated by the acquisition of Bramalea, another Canadian commercial real estate company, who also had large holdings of land for their residential building program. I don't know all of the details, but the outcome was that Trizec started to make large cutbacks in 1991 with many senior staff being laid off, including Mike, my boss; Jim, the leasing vice president; and Kevin, the controller. Fortunately I was spared with the encouraging words from the executive vice president that I was a "keeper".

However, as time went on, Trizec's fortunes dwindled, along with value of their stock, making my many stock options worthless. I could see the writing on the wall in late spring in 1993. In August, I was advised that I was to be laid off at the end of October. Because I had worked for the company for over 12 years — 16 years in total — I was to receive 12-months severance pay. Very generous I thought. I could take it in monthly installments or in one lump sum. At the time, I was very concerned that the company might not last another year, so I took the money in one lump sum.

It was now obvious that I needed to find suitable employment. I decided that while Michigan was a great place to live for eight months of the year, the months of January and February were extremely cold, and March and April were dreary, overcast, and wet. I decided that if I had to find myself a new job that it would be preferable to work in a state where the weather was mild and comfortable. Suzan ruled out the southern states because of the long, humid summers and the West Coast because it was too far away, the location of a lot of natural disasters, and the high cost of living. The situation was similar when we made the decision to emigrate. We poured over a map of the eastern United States and finally decided on Richmond, Virginia. It seemed that Richmond was a wonderful city, full of history and had a growing economy. It was close to Washington D.C. if we wanted a cultural experience, close to the Smoky Mountains and the Appalachian Trail if we wanted to absorb the beauty of nature or go hiking, and close to Virginia Beach if we wanted to hang out at the ocean. Our choice of Richmond was deliberate and resolute.

With our minds made up, we sold our house of 15 years in Troy. We sold it without a realtor at the highest price the neighborhood had ever achieved. We stored our best furniture, not knowing exactly where we were going to land, and took with us much of the furniture we had in our house on Lake Michigan in northern Michigan. We rented a very nice apartment in Midlothian in south Richmond, and I began the tedious task of finding myself a job. At a great cost (to someone out of work), I joined a company that specialized in helping senior managers and executives find suitable positions. The best the company did for me was to provide me the basic office requirements and get me out of the apartment. I applied to many companies that were advertising for qualified people to fill various positions, but they all fell on deaf ears. I wrote hundreds of letters and made numerous calls that were never returned, however hard I tried to get through to them.

There is no doubt in my mind that networking is by far the best way to find a job. After nine months of a very frustrating job search I called Jim, from the BOMA organization, who suggested that I call a particular senior executive at Insignia Commercial Group. Jim told me the company was growing rapidly, and they were looking for good people. Naturally I followed through on his advice, and the senior executive referred me to another executive in California who then told me to get in touch with Tex, a manager in Dallas. Apparently they had just fired a manager with a gambling problem who had been caught with his hand in the till.

I chatted with Tex about the position for a while. Although the job was not a perfect fit, I felt I could be an asset to the company — not to mention that I badly needed a job.

"Where would I be based?" I casually asked.

"Oh, in Detroit. We always like to hire people who have a good knowledge of city in which they are working," he replied.

You could have knocked me over with a feather. Was it possible that we were heading back to Detroit to face the harsh winters and our friends, who had so graciously given us a wonderful going away party?

I met with Tex and his manager in Dallas and was rather unimpressed by his demeanor, particularly the peculiar habit of chewing tobacco and constantly spitting out the residue. As an Englishman, I found this intensely distasteful. However, he was to be my boss if I was able to secure the job, so I just bit my lip.

In the meantime, I had made up my mind that Richmond was not a good place to find employment in the commercial real estate industry. There were little-to-no jobs in the offering and although we both found it to be a very pleasant place to live, I was unable to secure a job there.

However, I knew that Atlanta was a good market for employment, including the field of commercial real estate. Our plan was to move there.

I was anxious about my pending move, so I asked Tex if I had secured the job, whereupon he advised me that I had to interview with the Californian executive. It's like the CIA was about to employ me! I explained that I was about to move to Atlanta, but that I wouldn't if I knew that I had a reasonable chance of being employed by Insignia. He understood my plight, but he still relished in telling me that he could not help me. I had to get on with my life, and I could not rely on one possible job opportunity, so Suzan and I packed up the apartment, and with the help of U-Haul, moved to another apartment in northwest Atlanta. Again, it was a delightful apartment surrounded by beautifully kept grounds, backing onto a wooded area.

Insignia's headquarters was in Greenville, South Carolina, a difficult place to fly to directly. The Californian executive had to change planes in Atlanta in order to get to Greenville, so it was decided that he and I would meet at the airport for my final interview. I arrived early to survey the Delta terminal for an appropriate place for the interview. I found a new alteration/addition that was very elegantly appointed with large comfortable chairs and not at all crowded. A perfect place for an interview. I was to meet him off the plane, and I talked with the guys in Dallas to obtain a rough description of him. After about a minute of trying to explain what he looked like one of them said, "You can't miss him, he has a huge honker!"

They were right. I didn't miss him. We exchanged pleasantries and he announced that he was famished. We quickly found a food outlet where he purchased two hot dogs and a pretzel. In the café there was loud music playing on the speaker system and a guy slumped in the corner playing a totally different song on his guitar. We settled down at a greasy table where the interview started. He quickly hammered me with questions, while eating the hot dogs and pretzel, which I answered to the best of my ability. There was something specific that he was looking for but I was unable to satisfy him with the right answers. My surroundings were quite unsettling, and his questions were even more unsettling. There was so much that I had done in my career that I wanted to tell him, but he didn't seem to be interested. I don't recall how long this went on, but finally he said that he had a flight to catch. He thanked me, said goodbye, and disappeared. I was totally exhausted and didn't know what to think.

Tex called me a couple of days later to discuss the situation. His demeanor was disconcerting. He told me that the job was mine since they couldn't find anyone better. We discussed salary — $20,000 less than I was making at Trizec — and vacation time — two weeks a year. No amount of talking was going to change his stance, and I was in no position to bargain. This whole hiring process left a very bitter taste in my mouth that stayed with me for far too long.

Work at Insignia was stifling. Any new ideas that I presented were ruled out or, worse still, ignored. About 80 percent of the projects I proposed were carried out by some other developer and proved to be very successful. There were six separate people I reported to over the four years I was there. Although my reviews were good and my salary increases were generous in percentage terms, I was never content there. Overall, my staff was very competent, and I kept telling myself that I should be happy — I had a good paying job with little stress, a lot more than most people can say. But as far as senior and executive management direction, employee motivation, and job satisfaction goes, Insignia fell far short.

CHAPTER 33

RESIDENTIAL REAL ESTATE

I n late 1999, I found myself laid off for the second time in my career — Insignia had folded the Detroit region. With high stress resulting from a job loss and mounting debt, Dr. Jefferies felt that I would benefit from the services of a psychologist again. This time he referred me to Dr. Carolyn Baxter. I was delighted to be referred to a female, as I was sure she would better understand my issues. Dr. Baxter was an attractive and charming psychologist. At our first meeting, I was quick to tell her of my transsexual issues, and she advised me that she practiced a holistic approach to medicine. My heart sank, as I hadn't a clue what that meant. I didn't want to show my ignorance and just said "Ohh…" trailing off as I said it. I felt sure it had something to do with herbal medicine and was not thrilled about the prospects. But we carried on regardless. When I returned home, I immediately looked for a dictionary and then on my PC and was very relieved to learn that holistic medicine meant 'taking into account all of somebody's physical, mental, and social conditions in the treatment of illnesses'.

In my search for suitable employment, I carefully prepared my resume and applied to hundreds of jobs, again. I altered it a little each time to fit the particular job I was applying to, but all to no avail. Unfortunately, this time I did not have the help of a professional agency. 95 percent of my applications were never acknowledged and the few companies that kindly did, did so with a standard letter thanking me and carried on to say they would contact me if they needed me to come in for an interview. Even though I had extensive experience in my field, was highly qualified as an accountant and commercial property management and development, and had the good fortune to receive continuing education in many different management areas, I was never contacted. I came to the conclusion that there was a 'glass wall' for those applying who were over age 50, even though it is illegal. Of course it would be impossible to prove, but why would company hire me when they could hire someone 20 years younger at half my salary and train them in their methods and procedures? Would I have worked for a lesser salary? Certainly, but I never came close to that stage of a job search.

It was while discussing my job situation, or lack of it I should say, with Dr. Baxter, that she suggested that I look into residential real estate. A very good friend of hers was a realtor with a local company and was extremely successful. Since I already had a Michigan real estate license, she thought it would be a good idea for me to look into the possibilities. What she didn't know was that asking a commercial real estate person to go into residential real estate is like asking a Catholic if they would like to become a Muslim. I didn't know what to say to my kind doctor and as I didn't want to upset her and since I had no better suggestion, I agreed to look into it.

The interview was with the manager of the Bloomfield Hills office of Max Broock, a very successful, family-owned, local real estate company. It was established in 1895, and is one of the oldest, if not the oldest, real estate company in the United States. The meeting was rather mundane, but the people I met seemed to be very pleasant, and when I was offered a desk I accepted. Mind you, I later learned that anyone who wants to be a realtor would be accepted so long as they fit the mold.

So, now I started yet another career. The manager I interviewed with stepped down and was replaced with Jon, an ex-high school principal, who was high in energy and low in real estate experience. It always seemed to me that he was shooting from the hip at first, but with experience things improved. I found out that it takes time, money, and experience to become a successful realtor. I had plenty of the first and little of the other two, but

I somehow managed to scrape together a meager living in my first year. I could see how one could become successful and start to make a decent living, so I persevered. We were advised that teams work better than individuals, so I suggested to Suzan that she join me. She was apprehensive that she could pass the state licensing exam, but I knew she was more than capable and felt that we would make a good team.

Suzan passed the exam with ease, and we were given an office to share. We worked extremely well together and built a reasonably successful business with the help of our golden Labrador puppy, Mandy, who often shared our office and kept us sane during insane moments. The problem was that ever since I started residential real estate, the market in Michigan was sluggish, a 'buyers' market. I longed for a vibrant market such as California or Florida where business was fast and furious, and where real money was being made by realtors. But this was Michigan, driven by a flailing auto industry and managed by a next to useless legislative body and governor.

From everything I saw and read, things were going to get worse, much worse. Even though we had finally built up a reasonable business, homes were taking a long time to sell and prices seemed to me to be stagnant at best. It was 2005, and I had started to think about moving to a more active market. I now had my brokers' license and felt comfortable with my skill level to transport it to another state, even though we would both have to take the state licensing exam wherever we went. Florida was out, as Suzan had always said it was too hot for her, and California was too far from family and friends. I had read about Charlotte, North Carolina attracting banking business from New York, and from all I could garner, it seemed to have a good real estate market and was an agreeable place to live. I mentioned it to Suzan who listen intently but was non-committal.

The next day we started to talk about the possibility of moving again, and Suzan said in a matter of fact way, "If we are going to move, I am going to move to where our children are."

"Oh" I said somewhat surprised, "I hadn't even considered that."

I had been thinking only of the business side of the equation, but she had a good point. Why wouldn't we move to Massachusetts or Colorado?

"Well, where would you want to go?" I said, knowing it was a difficult question to answer because it would seem that we would be favoring one child over the other.

"I think we should go to Debbie and Julia because she is our only grandchild."

Can't argue that point, I thought, as my mind began to wander. Newport, Rhode Island, the home of U.S. sailing and an appealing, quaint town, is only about 45 minutes from Deb and Craig's home in Rehoboth, MA. Not too close and not too far. So I posed the idea of going to Newport, which Suzan thought was a good idea. Real estate there was reasonably good, from an agent's point of view, and so our minds were made up.

CHAPTER 34

ELECTROLYSIS

The move to Rhode Island was almost routine for us. The hard part was leaving our friends of 27 years. True, we had done it before only to return, and I suspect that some of them thought that it was going to happen again. We had the usual farewell parties, which are hard and gratifying at the same time, but going to live by Debbie and Julia made it much easier from our point of view. Deb had found for us a nice rental house in Middletown, a town adjacent to Newport, that could accommodate our large English dining room furniture and Mandy, our relatively new and large Labrador, two important criteria.

For me, the most tiresome part of each move is establishing new amenities and every day conveniences such as supermarkets, drug stores, radio and TV stations, doctors and dentists, tax advisors, attorneys, etc.

One of the first professionals I needed to find was an electrologist to continue removing my facial hair. From puberty on, I had a dark shadow on my face, and I absolutely detested shaving. And the fact I needed to shave every day, sometimes twice a day was awful. I started electrolysis to remove my whiskers in the early 90s with a wonderful electrologist named Martha. By the time I moved from Detroit she had completed the sides of my face. The process involves sticking a needle down into the follicle of an individual hair and passing an electric current to the base of the hair and then the hair is plucked out. If the hair grows back, which it's apt to do, the process is repeated. It's a slow and expensive process, but over time the face becomes free of hair. The electrolysis procedure is apparently the only known way of permanently removing hair, although I had laser hair removal carried out on my chest and stomach, and the hairs never grew back.

Eventually I found Kathleen Stone in East Providence. She sounded very nice and professional on the phone, so I made an appointment. My first appointment was easygoing and the chatter flowed. After several appointments, I'm not sure what we were discussing, but I felt it time to tell Katie that I was transsexual.

I'm uncertain if she was truly surprised or was acting but she said "Oh, really" in quite a surprised voice and let me know that she had several "trans" patients. Being the consummate professional, she checked with one patient before letting me know about Aveda. Aveda was a hairdresser, Portuguese from the Azores, and spoke perfect English. I met her at her hair salon, and we quickly became friends. We obviously had a lot in common, but she was quite beautiful and much more feminine than me. Everything I aspired to be. She later confided in me that her chromosomes were XXY, XX being female and XY being male, although recent studies suggest that it is not necessarily related to transsexualism. We went out together several times and she was always so kind and very helpful in so many ways. Not the least of which was to do my hair in the most beautiful fashions.

Katie kindly suggested that if I felt the need, I was welcome to come to her as a female. I jumped at the chance, wanting to express my female side at every opportunity. I always changed in a disused layby on the way to her and changed back before I went home. For me, it was a wonderful respite even if it was only for a couple of hours. Over the years, my friendship with Katie has grown, to the point that I now call her a close friend and try to meet up with her whenever I'm in her vicinity.

CHAPTER 35

MORE PSYCHIATRISTS

was still on my antidepressant medication and quickly needed to find a new psychiatrist. Without knowing anyone in Rhode Island, the internet and phone book quickly became my friends. It seemed that psychiatrists were few and far between in the Newport area. That was a good sign I thought. The first psychiatrist I called said he wasn't taking any new patients, and so I personally visited the second, and last psychiatrist, in the area with the hope that if he met me, he would like me and take me on. Negative on both counts. I caught him just as he was leaving for the day, and he had something much more important on his mind. My family's motto is "Perseverantia Vincit" — Latin for "Perseverance Conquers" — which is an excellent motto that I have tried to follow all my life. So back to the phone book and then the internet and since there was no psychiatrist in the immediate vicinity I expanded my search and found one in North Kingstown, Rhode Island, about a 40-minute drive from my house. I called Dr. Silverman who said she would be happy to have me as a patient, and I was elated: she was a female psychiatrist, and she was willing to take me on. She told me that my initial visit would be three hours long and cost $600. Wow! I told her that I was already under treatment in Michigan and didn't think that I needed such an extensive first assessment. She advised me that all her patients have to participate in this process, otherwise she could not take them on. Feeling that I had little choice at this point, I agreed.

Driving over the beautiful Pell suspension bridge on my way to my first appointment with Dr. Silverman, I felt a little disgruntled that I was not only having to drive 40 minutes to my doctor's appointment, but that I also had to pay $600 for what was ostensibly a visit to obtain a prescription for the medication I needed. But it had to be done — I knew what I was like without it: moody, irritable, depressed, dour, and withdrawn.

Dr. Silverman was everything I expected: slim, sprightly, and professional. We started off with the usual questions and answers and then got into a more detailed discussion of various aspects of my life. About an hour and a half into the session I found myself tearing up, which then turned into full blown crying. But I had no idea why! Dr. Silverman remained silent for a bit and then said in a concerned way, "What's wrong?"

I shook my head and mumbled while still sniffling, "I don't know."

After about another minute of allowing me to compose myself, she continued, "We seem to have hit a nerve."

"Yes," I nodded.

I took a deep breath and stopped crying. I truthfully told her that I couldn't understand why I was teary. She probed deeper, and after a short while I said, "Maybe it has something to do with the fact that I'm transsexual."

Dr. Silverman then explained to me the cause of transsexualism as she understood it. All fetuses start off as females, which is why males have nipples. During the first trimester, the sex of a fetus is determined. It is during this period that something goes awry. Her technical explanation became too difficult for me to understand. But, I am convinced that something happens prior to birth that determines if one is transsexual or not. I was brought up in a very male way but had this overwhelming desire from the beginning to be female. Frankly, I don't understand it. There have been numerous theories and just as many studies but the answer has yet to be determined.

After telling her, I felt another load lifted from my shoulders. To be honest, I can't even remember what was said after that: the three hours seemed to pass quickly, and I was mentally and emotionally exhausted. We were winding down our conversation when I was totally caught off guard. It was a life changing point in time, a moment when my heart literally skipped a beat, and all my senses jumped to life.

Quietly and in a matter of fact sort of way, Dr. Silverman said, "If you wish to make the change, I would be happy to help you."

I couldn't believe my ears. For 20 years I have been talking to psychiatrists and psychologists. Not once had any of them offered me help in this manner. They were all busy trying to prevent any change by giving me drugs, hypnosis, mental therapy and all but ignored my primary problem. I was so shocked and excited by the thought that I was momentarily dumbfounded. My initial thought was to shout YES! YES! YES! But then decided that I should at least show a little self-control and some thought into this major life changing decision. As I struggled to say something, Dr. Silverman added, "I have helped another patient through the change, and she is doing very well."

"Thank you, Doctor. I really appreciate your offer — it means a great deal to me. I will definitely give it some serious thought and let you know." It was really hard to hide my exuberance, and I am sure she felt it.

"Okay, we need to set up your next appointment," she said smiling at me and opening up her calendar. My mind was racing about the possibilities that our conversation had just unleashed. Then I suddenly remembered something.

"Oh, Doctor! What about my medication?"

"What about your medication?" she replied seemingly rather annoyed.

"Well," I said, feeling somewhat exasperated. "The reason I came to you was to fill my current prescriptions for the Depakote, Wellbutrin, and Lexapro that I'm currently taking."

"All right," she said, "Umm," pausing a little while she thought, "you know, I don't think you need all these drugs. Which one are you out of?"

"Depakote," I said, maybe a little too sternly.

"Okay, I'll give you a one-month prescription for Depakote," she continued, "but we'll discuss your medication at your next appointment next week. Is the same time all right? Oh! We have the holidays coming up, how about January 4, 2006. Wow! We are already into 2006. Is that okay with you?"

"Oh, no!" I started to protest, "There's no need for me to see you next month. In Michigan I saw my psychiatrist every three months."

"That may be so", she said, "but we need to finish our discussion today, and we need to sort out your medication. I'll put you down for two hours." I reluctantly agreed. I didn't mind the visits or discussing my issues, especially if she going to help me with a possible change. It was the cost that was troubling me: at a rate of $210 an hour I could see my funds rapidly disappearing. I could feel myself getting into a vise-like grip that I would have difficulty getting out of.

"If you like," she said, "you are welcome to come to your next appointment dressed as a woman." Again, you could have knocked me over with a feather. Before I could react she asked if I had a a female name.

"Well, yes," I said rather shyly. "It's Sarah." This question had been running through my mind over the years, and I had thought about several names including Victoria (Vickie), Louise, Stephanie, and Anne and had discarded them all for one reason or another before finally settling on Sarah. I have always liked the name Sarah and have never met a Sarah I didn't like. It was age appropriate and my great-grandmother's name. I've always felt it important for a person to choose an age appropriate name. A 60-year-old trans woman with the first name Taylor or Brittany seems so odd to me, and a flag to any unsuspecting person.

"Okay, Sarah. I'll see you on January 4th" the doctor said smiling at me, closing her calendar. I could feel myself blushing but pleased that she called me by my female name.

Finally, after nearly six decades, I found someone who was ready and willing to help me. It was hard for me to believe that it was actually happening. There was absolutely no doubt in my mind that I wanted to go through with it. I just had to think through all the implications.

First there were my children, Deb was 35 years old and her daughter, Julia only 1. Jeremy was 32 years old, and both were married. I felt the children were of an age where they could handle such dramatic news, and my only grandchild was too young to know any different. I wasn't sure how Suzan would react, but I really wanted her to stay with me, and it was quite common for wives of male-to-female transsexuals to stay with them. I could only hope.

Suzan was very tolerant of my increasingly odd behavior, both my depressive state and desire to be all things female. What incredible stress I put her under. I genuinely felt guilty, but my depressions and transsexual feelings were both out of my control. That was the way I was built!

With my mind made up, I thought about what effect it would have on the other members of my family and all the friendships I have made over the years. I was sure that almost everyone would be shocked beyond words but would be accommodating for the most part. There were some "friends" I was certain that I would lose, as they were so little-minded they would be unable to handle the news, and some of my more macho friends would drop by the wayside. So be it. But my close family would, I was sure, stand by me.

At the next session with Dr. Silverman, there was another person, a psychologist, also present. Dr. Silverman had called me previously to ask if I minded having another professional present in the room as an observer, as there was a possibility that the person would be joining Dr. Silverman in some capacity or other. To be frank, I couldn't have cared less — all I wanted was the medication and to discuss the possibility of a transition. If this would expedite the matter, so be it.

The session continued where we left off, discussing my transsexual feelings. I told her almost immediately that I had given much thought to her offer of helping with a full transition.

"Doctor," I said quietly, "I have decided that I really want to go through with the change."

"Oh," she said, "that's wonderful! I'll help you through the process in every way I can." And so the next session continued and the questions started.

"Did you ever dress up?"

"Yes, from a very early age."

"How often?"

"Whenever I felt a desperate need, although it was not always possible."

"Yes, I understand, but how many times a month? Did you go out in public? Does Suzan know? How does she react when you do this?"

The questions kept coming, and I answered each one thoughtfully and truthfully.

"Have you ever had sex with a man?"

"Good heavens, no! I'm transsexual, not homosexual."

"Have you ever thought about having sex with a man?" she continued in a soothing voice.

"No, I haven't," I again answered truthfully.

"Have you ever taken female hormones?"

"Well, yes," I said feeling rather vulnerable all of a sudden.

"What were the hormones and who prescribed them?"

"Okay," I said breathing out in an audible and resigned manner. "The hormones were Premarin, and they weren't prescribed."

"So how did you manage to get them?" Dr. Silverman quizzed.

"Well, when I was Director of Operations in Detroit, one of the buildings had many medical practices as tenants. I use to go into an OB/GYN office with the pretense of checking on the cleaning of the suite. They used to keep a large cardboard box on the floor filled with samples that had been given to the physicians by visiting salesmen. I knew that these samples were not accounted for in any way, so I used to help myself to some Premarin. I didn't see it as being too dishonest, as the physicians received them for free and were going to either give them away or throw them away."

Dr. Silverman made no judgment. She simply asked me if they had any effect on me.

"Very little," I responded, "I really didn't take them in sufficient quantities or on a consistent basis. But they made me feel quite feminine; maybe it was a placebo effect."

"Okay, with regards to the depression medications you are on, what I would like to do is to ease you off each one individually and see how you get on. If you find yourself having an adverse reaction, you can go back on. What do you think?"

Thinking of the reduced cost of medication, I readily agreed. She decided that I should slowly come off Depakote and then if that worked out, then I should slowly come off Wellbutrin and finally Lexapro. We had a plan.

As the session came to a close and I was paying her bill, I was thinking of my drive back to Middletown. She chirped up, "Wow! This is going to be quite a journey."

"Oh no, it's not too bad. Only about 20 minutes the other side of the bridge," I replied.

Dr. Silverman burst out laughing, "No, I meant your life's journey!"

Laughing at myself, I had to agree.

The drug plan was working until it came time to give up Lexapro, which I was loath to do. I knew from past experience that I needed something if I was going to stay sane. Dr. Silverman agreed to my request, and I still take it today with no side effects.

After a few sessions, she suggested that Suzan accompany me so that she could judge the situation at home, which in my mind was okay. Suzan reluctantly agreed to go and was pretty quiet on the drive there — unusual for Suzan. When the session started I was in for a shock. Suzan was extremely volatile and angry with Dr. Silverman pushing me towards having the operation. This, of course, was very unfair, but no attempt by me was going to change her mind. The session ended with absolutely nothing accomplished.

As suggested, future visits to the psychiatrist were dressed as a woman. At first, it was quite unnerving to go out in public as I first did at Katie's, but the more I did it, the more confident I became. However terrible I might have looked from the outside, I felt wonderful inside.

Another outlet for me was when I went out with Aveda. We went to a couple of Portuguese restaurants, and she was always fun to be around. She was very elegant and it was hard to imagine that she was ever male, unlike me. However inadequate I felt, she was able to build up my confidence. In one discussion we were talking about the operation. She told me that a Dr. Kunaporn in Phuket, Thailand did hers.

"Oh, really," I said. "Why didn't you have it done in the U.S.?"

"Well, first of all," she started, "it's so much less expensive in Thailand, and the doctors are probably more advanced in this area of medicine. The hospitals are really great, and whereas here they'll kick you out in a couple of days, over there you stay for two weeks. And the nursing care is amazing. I was one of the first to have a new procedure done by Dr. Kunaporn, and it's been wonderful, I'll have to show you sometime what he did for me. You'll need to go on his website to check him out."

"Wow," I said excitedly, "how do you spell his name?"

She spelled out Sanguan Kunaporn. I wasn't even home more than two minutes when I was on the internet checking out his website.

This is what is says today:

> *Male to Female Gender Reassignment Surgery (also known as Sex Reassignment Surgery, or SRS) is a complex and irreversible sex change operation and therefore prospective patients must demonstrate a firm commitment to the decision to proceed.*
>
> *The World Professional Association for Transgender Health (formerly the Harry Benjamin Association) recommends that six objectives must be met before a sex change operation is undertaken.*

- *The patient must demonstrate a desire for sexual reassignment for at least two years prior to surgery.*

- *A clinical behavioral scientist trained to deal specifically with transsexualism must make the diagnosis of Gender Identity Disorder.*

- *The patient must live and work exclusively in his or her chosen gender for not less than 12 months.*

- *The patient must be under psychological or psychiatric care for not less than six months prior to surgery.*

- *The patient must have commenced hormonal sex reassignment treatment for not less than six months prior to surgery.*

- *Throughout the evaluation process, peer reviews must be evaluated and the patient discussed by the appropriate clinicians.*

In order to preserve the integrity and ethics of Transgender Reassignment Surgery, the Medical Council of Thailand now insists that all prospective patients are approved by a Thai psychiatrist. To facilitate this process, Doctor Sanguan requires, one month before intended surgery, a letter of referral from a psychiatrist, a physician, an endocrinologist or a psychotherapist. This needs to demonstrate the person's suitability for GRS and will help ensure that the examination by the local psychiatrist (which will take place on the day prior to scheduled surgery) does not cause a delay to the surgery schedule. If the patient can meet these criteria, they will be scheduled for operation. Doctor Sanguan performs GRS in two stages, separated by seven days, a unique and proven process designed to improve appearance and sensitivity. For this reason, and to aid recovery, patients can expect to spend three to four weeks in Phuket.

Dr. Sanguan Kunaporn is affectionately known as Dr. Sanguan. Most of what is on his website today is the same as it was in 2006, except there was no mention of living and working in one's chosen gender for 12 months. I was definitely not living or working as a female, at least not outwardly. Of course, in my mind I've been working and living as a female all my life. Nowadays, in the United States, a transsexual has to live as a female for two years before they will perform the surgery.

It's important to understand that there are some who seek Sex (Gender) Reassignment Surgery (SRS) or (GRS) that are not transsexual but feel that their lives would be better as a female. This is not a good reason to undergo SRS. Although there are differences of opinion, in my mind a transsexual is one who wholly identifies as the opposite sex and is totally disgusted by their own genitals. End of story. There are many other forms of transgender (as opposed to transsexual) such as transvestites, pretty boys, drag queens, bigender, gender benders, she-males, etc. Generally speaking these individuals are not good candidates for SRS.

One of the stipulations dictates that a patient must undergo hormonal sex reassignment treatment for six months prior to surgery. I had been doing that for considerably longer than six months, but it was self-administered. I had read on the internet (site now discontinued) what I needed to take and in what quantities, so I ordered the appropriate medication though a foreign website. Amazingly, and probably stupidly, I have never had an endocrinologist. To this day, I still administer my own medication both for depression and hormonal issues.

It was now the summer of 2006, and I started corresponding with Dr. Sanguan. His secretary filled me in with all the requirements, most of which I already knew from either Aveda or his website. The one thing that I needed and was concerned about was a letter from Dr. Silverman saying that I was a suitable candidate for SRS. At my next session I brought up the issue of the letter. She said she would be happy to do it but it would cost $200. I thought that was a little outrageous, and I think she sensed it. "It requires a great deal of thought and professional input," she explained. I let it go at that.

Mentally, I was now committed to the surgery and thought it was time to tell Suzan. How was she going to take the news? Maybe she would just explode and walk out. Maybe she would rant and rave for a while and then start sobbing. Maybe she would give me the silent treatment. But I knew Suzan and knew that none of these things were going to happen. Yes, she loved me just as I adored her, but she also knew of all my issues and troubles. And so, when I told her it was an anticlimactic event. She took the news quietly. My mind is totally blank as to what she said and I think her mind is too. There was a sort of numbness in the air, a resignation that all the things she had tried to prevent, mainly for the sake of the children, were now occurring. I'm sure the words of Dr. Jones, my early psychologist were ringing in her ears. "It's very hard to watch your husband slowly slip away." In my case it was very slow and probably more painful because of it.

At my next session with Dr. Silverman, two things of importance happened. First, she announced that she was closing her practice in Rhode Island — she and her husband were moving to New Mexico to settle there and set up a new practice. My only concern was that she produce the letter of recommendation I needed for Dr. Sanguan. She looked sort of anguished, so I suggested that I write it for her and she sign it. This she readily agreed to, so I put pen to paper.

Dear Dr. Kunaporn,

Sarah Lynne Hartley has been under my care since December of 2005. She is an extraordinary well-balanced person who thrives in her female role and has her own real estate business. It is my professional opinion, without reservation, that Ms. Hartley would greatly benefit from sexual reassignment surgery.

Sincerely,

Debra J. Silverman. M.D.

On my next visit I presented her with the letter and she said in a surprised voice, "Oh! Is that all I have to say?"

"I believe so," I answered "and if you wouldn't mind just signing and faxing it to him that would be terrific."

"I'll be happy to do that for you," she replied. No money changed hands!

In my correspondence with Dr. Sanguan, we had tentatively set the date for my surgery as March 23, 2007. There was a huge feeling of relief within me. At my next hair appointment with Aveda, I excitedly told her that I had my surgery booked. She was really happy for me and asked if I would like to see the results of her operation.

"Well yes, that would be wonderful," I replied anxious to know how I was going to look and feel in few months. So we trotted off to the bathroom where she promptly lifted up her skirt and proceeded to show me. "Wow! That's wonderful," I said as I gave her genitals a thoroughly good look. All rather surreal. When we went back into the salon I asked her all sorts of questions, like was her clitoris sensitive and did she have orgasms and was her vagina wet when she had intercourse. The first two questions were answered positively, but the last she said was easily fixed with the help of KY jelly or something similar.

Over the years I had kept in touch with several of my Trizec colleagues, now considered friends. One such friend was Christina, the attorney. She was bright, fun, and energetic. Both Suzan and I got on well with her and her partner, Lynne. I was excited with my developing plan and decided to tell Chris about it. She was very surprised, as most people are when I tell them, and supportive. A few days later she called and was interested in hearing more details. I told her my plans and that I was having the operation in Phuket, Thailand on March 23.

"Oh my goodness," she exclaimed. "That's my birthday!"

"Well it seems that we might be sharing a birthday," I quipped.

We both laughed. Chris asked me if Suzan was going with me and I said that she wasn't. Then she asked if anyone was going to be with me for the operation and I told her no, but that was okay with me.

True to form, Chris called me again and suggested that she and Lynne would like to be with me. They had discussed it and felt I should have some sort of support when in Thailand and that they would like to do that, as well as to have a holiday in Thailand. That was music to my ears, as I knew that going through an operation of the type I was considering was monumental and that any support would be fantastic.

The stage was set, but there were a few other things that had to be addressed, the main one being an official name change. I researched Rhode Island law and it seemed a fairly simple procedure. I had to fill out and submit a load of forms and wait to be called in front of a local judge in the Probate court. Also, I had to place a notice in the local paper. Eventually, my hearing date was set, and I went to court in my best female garb.

The day arrived in December 2006, and I sat patiently in the courtroom. Eventually my name was called, and I went up to the judge. What I thought should have been an easy and routine procedure was not. He started interrogating me as to why I wanted to change my name and in a short span of time denied my application. I was flabbergasted. He told me that if I came back in six months he would reconsider my application. I was totally dumbstruck. I stormed out of the courtroom to the ladies room and bawled my eyes out. This is so ridiculous and narrow minded I thought. After about 10 minutes, I managed to compose myself to the point I could go to my car. I sat there for a little while and was so very mad. I decided to go back into the courtroom and confront the judge again. He saw me reappear and waited until all his cases had been administered and then called me to his bench.

"What do you want now?" he demanded.

"I want to know why you denied my request for a name change."

"Well, how do I know if you are not doing this just escape your creditors?"

"Escape my creditors!" I said incredulously. "Do you think I would go through with years of psychological testing and schedule a sex change operation to be a woman just to escape my creditors? That's absolutely ridiculous."

"Come back and see me in six months and I'll reconsider your application," is all he could say.

"Well, what about my flights to Thailand which are booked in the name of Sarah Hartley."

"That's something out of my control and you'll have to sort out." I was about to throttle him for the second time that day.

My flights were booked from Boston to Kennedy airport in New York and then a nonstop Thai Air flight to Bangkok. Surprisingly the airlines were very accommodating and after seeing documentation, changed the name on my flights. Phew! One aggravation out of the way. Maybe this was all for the better — now I didn't have to change my passport for the trip. But I still planned to travel as a female and the authorities could figure out whatever they wanted to figure out!

The myriad of pieces were finally coming together, with exception of one thing. Other than Suzan, Chris, and Lynne, no one knew what I was about to do. I really thought my children should be aware. So one weekend afternoon, when I knew that Deb would be home, I went over to her house and after the small talk I sat her down in her living room. Of course she was wide eyed and stunned as I told her how I felt and what I was going to do. Her poor husband Craig, having no idea what we were discussing came waltzing into the room, all cheery, and Deb sent him on his way saying that we were in the middle of a very important discussion. I felt so sorry for him.

Then there was Jeremy. He was living in Boulder, Colorado with Erin his wife. I couldn't go there for several reasons and felt that a phone call would not be the best way. I thought that a letter, explaining what I was going to do and why, would be the best way. Right or wrong, it turned out badly. He was really confused and very angry.

As an internet guru, he was immediately on the world wide net asking for information and suggestions. A psychiatrist in Australia had the same issues, and his father had moved to a different part of the country and the psychiatrist was doing everything he could to stay in touch. He suggested that our family go to a psychologist in Rhode Island that he knew of, named Dr. Helga Mettler.

Jeremy and Deb made the appointment, and Suzan and I arrived at the appointed time. Personally, I was not sure what this was going to achieve but was happy to go along with the plan to help my children understand. Everybody voice their opinions, but little was achieved. I think everybody had the same opinion as when they went in. Jeremy was definitely the most concerned and raised some valid points, namely that I hadn't lived as a woman, which is required by many doctors before surgery. But my mind was made up.

After the meeting I wrote to Dr. Mettler:

Dear Helga,

I just wanted to thank you so much for taking time on your weekend to meet with my family. We all found the meeting very helpful and really appreciate your understanding and guidance. Anytime we can get to-

gether to talk and air our opinions about this difficult matter is time well spent.

It really pains me to see my family so traumatized by my actions, and I am constantly questioning my course. However, in the end I believe my surgery is the best course, and I feel that over time the children will have their fears and concerns minimized. They have known for only one month, and I am hoping that time will be a good healer in this case. I am most worried about Jeremy and intend to be constantly in touch with him. Debbie has been incredible, and in my opinion, will be fine. Suzan puts on a very brave face and hardly ever lets her feelings come through, which is not good. However, once in a while she breaks down for a minute or two, which I feel relieves the pressure a bit. She has said to me it is like a death in the family, but although she is resisting right now I want to stay as close as possible to her.

I will let you know how things go and will probably want to come and see you when I return from Thailand. Again, very many thanks for your help.

Kind regards,
Sarah Hartley (Peter Bamford)

She replied:

Dear Sarah: Well, that's different. How did you settle on that name? Are you honoring someone in that way? If so, that individual can be proud.

Peter, I am so glad that you all gained some understanding and peace; it will take time and patience, not just for them but also for you as you enter these never before chartered waters.

Yes, Jeremy has a difficult time. He is brave that he'll admit to it rather than trying to appease you. Actually, that speaks well of you as his father. My concerns are also for Suzan. She is a trooper, looks like she is made of steel. However, looks are deceiving and I don't think that she fools any of her family members. If she would want to speak to me in the future, of course I'll be available to her. She gave up her life dreams and must find the courage to redefine them for herself in due time.

Yes, I agree, Deb is a very remarkable daughter and will be able to sort it out in time. You did so well offering each one to take as long as is needed and to arrive at conclusions that will support their individual processes of tolerance, acceptance, and love evolve in time.

Peter, I wish you well. You are a remarkable individual. On my web page I have Robert Frost's poem "The road less traveled". To you to go the road less taken will (make…) all the difference."

I found this quote and with your permission I want to mail it to you for support:

"We may become aware that worldly concerns and distractions keep us trapped in samara,

And we may feel an intense desire to be liberated from it. Then we find ourselves at the meeting point

Of two paths: one leads to liberation, and the other to the lesser destinies of samara."

Dilgo Khyentse Rinpoche
Be well, and peaceful. Helga

The stress of the last six months was beginning to show. Although I should be elated that I was finally on my way to womanhood, I was depressed. Nothing new there, but it felt deeper. I was so torn between my lifelong desire to be female and my deep love for Suzan. I knew in my own mind the two were not compatible and was really tormented. She had not said anything to me about a divorce, but I knew in my heart that if I went through with my plans, it was inevitable. I sat at the kitchen table in our Middletown house, sobbing, with my head on the table shielded by my arms.

"I don't know what to do. I just don't know what to do. What should I do?" My mind was in total turmoil. Suzan was there but didn't say a word, one way or the other. I think she was as tormented as I was. I'm sure on one hand she wanted the very best for me, but on the other she wanted me to remain a man, her husband. It was a truly awful moment in time affecting both of us, and my entire making.

The next day I felt no better. I was trying to carry out my real estate business but couldn't. I started driving around as I used to in the old days. I didn't know where I was going or why, I just kept driving and thinking and driving. I found myself driving up the Pell suspension bridge in Newport, crying so hard I could hardly see where I was going. This is it; this whole mess needs to end. I'm so tired of the pain. The pain I'm causing everyone I love and myself, it just has to stop. I can't take it anymore. I'm going to jump. Nobody can stop me now. I'm so bloody tired of this whole life. What's the point? I'm at the top of the bridge now, I have to stop, there's someone on my tail wondering why I'm slowing down. He's tailgating me. I have to continue. Now I'm past the top of the bridge. Oh hell, I'm going down the bridge and have to pay the toll at the end. Still sobbing, I find my money and pay. Who cares? Yes, who bloody well cares?

Well, as it turns out, many people care. Some don't but most do. And I'm so very thankful that I had a tailgater going over the bridge. I'm so glad I didn't jump to a certain death.

When I felt better and was able to think logically again, I reasoned that I had come so far and that there really was no option for me. I, all my life, had this overwhelming desire to live and work as a female, and I was just 10 weeks away from achieving this. I wasn't about to throw it all away at this point. The sun was setting on my manhood. The final pieces of the puzzle were now in place.

PART 7

A COMPLETE CHANGE

CHAPTER 36

THE SURGERY

Suzan had come to terms with my decision and was being very helpful. We went shopping together to get some necessities for my trip and discussed how I would travel as Peter Bamford on the way to her sex change operation.

Of course, my outfit was very gender neutral. Suzan drove me to the airport. No dramatics, no crying, no regrets by either person. Just a warm goodbye, and I was on my way. My flight from JFK to Bangkok was extraordinary. It was a nonstop flight on the most beautiful day. I could clearly see the different places as I flew over them: Norway, Sweden, Finland, Russia, the Middle East, and Asia. I had no idea an airliner could fly for 18 hours. At the Bangkok airport I found my flight to Phuket with no trouble. The surgeon's driver met me at the airport and was to take me to my hotel by the hospital. He told me in broken English that he had to wait for his "Doghter." I was a little perturbed that after 24 hours of travel that I had to wait so that he could pick up his daughter, but then I was in no position to argue, so we just waited and waited and eventually his phone rang. A discussion in Thai followed, then he smiled at me and said that was his "Doghter." Good, now I can get to my hotel and hopefully to sleep, I thought. Well, his Doghter turned out to be my doctor! Dr. Sanguan and I had a good chat for the 30 minute ride to my hotel. I felt privileged to have had such a good talk with the doctor before my surgery.

I found that with all the long flights, my internal clock was so messed up that it didn't know what time it was. I slept through the night and woke in the morning feeling really refreshed. Breakfast on the patio seemed to be in order, where the eternal Englishman in me ordered egg, sausage, and beans. The only thing I recognized was the fried egg. What the hell did I expect in Thailand. Duh!

The hospital where I was having my surgery was an international hospital, so most of the staff spoke English. They were so pleasant and kind that it was sort of unreal. The nurse who took me to my room didn't speak much English but was very caring and understanding. I felt very much at ease. The sex reassignment surgery (SRS) section was billed as being in an ideal setting: quiet, overlooking gardens and fountains. Unfortunately, they were building something next door and the gardens and fountains were being used as a staging area and were crawling with trucks. Well, who cares; I was to be lying in bed for the next 2 weeks.

Dr. Sanguan came to my room to announce that the original day of my surgery was unavailable and wanted to know if I would mind moving the surgery to tomorrow, March 22nd. I didn't mind one bit — the sooner the better, even if it was not going to be on Christina's birthday. To me it meant one day less of living this horrible lie. He checked me out, showing disappointment that I had been circumcised. I guess that part is useful.

The nurses arrived with medication, which I'm sure was to keep me calm and give me a good night's sleep. I had heard of patients the night prior to their SRS looking longingly at their penis or masturbating in front of a mirror for the last time. As far as I am concerned, those patients should not be having SRS. It never entered my mind to look lovingly at my penis or to masturbate; the sooner it was gone the happier I would be. Only hours remained.

The next morning, the gurney arrived. The male nurses lifted me onto it thinking, I'm sure, that this was the heaviest SRS patient that they had to deal with, but that was their problem not mine. After all, I was an ex-rugby player.

As I was wheeled to the operating room, two thoughts crossed my mind. The first was that the ceiling tiles were somewhat grungy and needed to be replaced; once a property manager, always a property manager, I guess. The other thought I had was how nice it was to have corridors open to the outside. Fresh air and sunshine were pouring in. Not once did I question my decision. On the contrary, it was a very relaxed, thank God it is finally going to happen moment.

When I came around my whole body was violently shaking. I heard a mumbling of voices and then a very thin blanket was placed over me. I immediately started to warm up and the shaking reduced and eventually stopped. The blanket was a type used for hypothermia patients and it certainly worked for me. The operating rooms are kept purposely cold to reduce germs and infections, I think, but my body didn't like it. I felt at peace and drifted off to netherland.

I awoke the next morning feeling numb. A nurse came to see me and asked how I was.

"Fine, thank you." I calmly replied. I was never stuck with "Oh! Now I'm a girl" or "Where is it?" Everything seemed so natural. No panics or worries, just a very relaxed feeling. Dr. Sanguan came to see me and said that everything went extremely well, that I just needed to rest. So rest I did. The surgery is a 2-part surgery. The first part is to remove the penis and scrotum and make a vagina and clitoris. The second stage is to line the vagina with the skin of the scrotum, which undergoes a de-hairing procedure. Many post-op girls had complained of hair growing in their vagina in the past, and Dr. Sanguan used a procedure that prevented this from happening. Basically the skin from the scrotum is scraped free of all hair follicles and is placed back in the vagina one week later. Just amazing!

Chris and Lynne arrived a week after my initial surgery and a day after my second surgery. I was really looking forward to seeing them, as I knew that they were arriving on Friday. But Friday came and went, and there was no sign of them. Saturday morning I was full of expectations, and they didn't show. The worst thoughts crossed my mind, totally unreasonable as I write this, but at the time I was emotional and concerned. I was concerned that they had a problem with their travel arrangements or they didn't care about my situation. Mid-afternoon, Chris poked her head around the door, and I burst into tears. She and Lynne were both surprised by my reaction.

Chris said, "I hope those are tears of joy at seeing us!"

I couldn't possibly explain my feelings.

At the end of my second week I was free to leave the hospital. The doctor's chauffeur took me to my hotel, which looked just fine with a pool and an endearing owner. The only issue I had were the bugs I encountered in my bathroom. They were small, gnat-like bugs, and they were everywhere. I had the energy and will power to get rid of every single one of them. I knew that complaining would mean moving rooms, and who knows what else I might find. It was better to stay where I was, right by the pool.

Chris and Lynne were in Phuket to help me through a somewhat traumatic experience, but they were also on holiday. I selfishly forgot about the second part, and so when they naturally went off on day trips I felt slighted. This played on my mind and when combined with the lack of my Lexapro while in hospital, I became depressed. One late afternoon when Chris and Lynne returned, Chris called me and found me to be very despondent. She quickly walked up the steep hill from her hotel to mine to comfort me. That's what I call a true friend: so very caring above it all. I don't know about them, but I was so relaxed being with them. Eating out every night, giggling and laughing and generally enjoying ourselves. Above all, I was the female I had always wanted to be.

Like all good things, the holiday came to an end. Chris and Lynne left while I stayed for a final checkup with Dr. Sanguan. Not knowing what I was going to do on my own for a few days, I told the hotel manager and part-owner that if there was anything I could do to help, I would be happy to do so. As it so happened, they were having a large party the next night, so she said that I could definitely be of assistance to them. That was terrific, thinking that I would be moving tables or cleaning up around the pool.

The day arrived and the owner asked if I would help Chompoo arrange the flowers! Oh my! Well I've arranged flowers in a vase quite successfully before, but Chompoo had some grand ideas. He wanted every column and every sconce to have a dramatic arrangement with white lilies and palms draping from them. Phew! Well, I said I would help and help I did. What could they do if they didn't like what I had done, deport me? As it happened, the arrangements looked really good, maybe even fantastic. Okay, my first arrangement wasn't that terrific, but by the third I was a real Constance Spry. The party was that night, and I decided to go out and have a real Thai meal at an off-the-beaten-track Thai restaurant. As I was walking out, the host of the party beckoned me over. He thanked me for the floral arrangements, to which I suggested that he should be thanking Chompoo. Oh no, he insisted, you did the most stellar work and would I join them in their party. As he was obviously English by birth, as was his partner, I felt comfortable and accepted his kind offer. It was a party celebrating his parent's 50th wedding anniversary, and they were such a lovely couple. The party was wonderful, and he had friends coming from all over including Australia, Singapore, and Hong Kong. The entertainment was a singing drag troupe, which, although well done, was really a turn off for me. Strangely, I just cannot stand that sort of act. I don't know why, it just really grates on me. Maybe it's because everything is always exaggerated.

CHAPTER 37

YOU'RE FIRED!

S uzan met me at Boston airport and was genuinely pleased to see me. I was dressed in a much more feminine outfit than when I left. I was more confident with a letter in hand from Dr. Sanguan stating the following:

Post-Operative Medical Certificate

April 3, 2007

This is to certify that Sarah Hartley; Previous name: Peter Frank Bamford HN. 50-06951, was admitted to this hospital since March 21, 2007. She underwent irreversible two-stage male to female sex reassignment surgery on March 22 and 29, 2007 at Phuket International Hospital, Phuket, Thailand. The surgery was successfully completed. All male genitalia including gonads have been removed and Sarah Hartley now has the female external genitalia that include labia major, labia minor, clitoris, and vaginal canal. She may now assume female gender.

Yours sincerely,
Sanguan Kunaporn, MD
Thai Cert. Board of Plastic & Reconstructive Surgery

The passport control officer looked at my picture and then a little quizzically at me. I just said that things change, to which he said, "I guess so," and I was on my way. My fears of being in real agony during the flight did not materialize, as the good doctor had given me some excellent painkillers.

Back at Rhode Island Coastal Homes, my new residential real estate company, and The Residences at Brown & Howard Wharf, the Newport condominiums Suzan and I were selling, I continued as Peter Bamford. Suzan felt strongly that announcing my change would benefit nothing, and I reluctantly agreed. So for work purposes I remained Peter Bamford, and for all other purposes I was Sarah Hartley. It was not a satisfactory way of living.

One day, the son of one of the partners came to our office and announced that the two partners had decided to sell their share of the condominium project to another developer and he (the son) was to remain as a partner. I asked him if he was happy at this arrangement and he told me he was extremely happy. But as with all change in senior management, there is a change of culture. This should have been for the better, but it wasn't. From the onset my new boss, Stacey, wanted her own people in place, which is not unusual. Suzan and I did not have a contract and therefore she could have just come to us and asked us to go. But instead she made our lives miserable by cutting us out of the decision making process and asking her secretary to sell the condos alongside us. The secretary at the time didn't even have a real estate salesperson license.

It was obvious what was going on and I had several customers on the cusp of signing. These multi-million dollar sales would have meant substantial commission for us, so when I saw her coming to my office with a low-level manager, I knew what was coming. They waltzed into the conference room and asked Suzan and I to join them. Smiling, she said that the company was undergoing some cost cutting measures and that unfortunately "the management" had decided that we should go. I let her ramble on for a few minutes and but I wasn't going to let her off lightly.

"Excuse me," I interrupted.

"Yes, Peter?"

"Let me see if I understand you correctly, you need to cut costs?"

"Yes," she said.

"So, you want to replace Suzan and me, two experienced real estate sales people, who know the project intimately well, and who are working on a commission-only basis with one less experienced sales person who would be salaried and have a commission. That does not seem like a cost cutting measure to me!"

The smile quickly dropped off her face and she blurted, "I'm just trying to make it easy for you!"

"I think you are trying to make it easy on yourself," I replied. "Come on Suzan, we've apparently outstayed our welcome," and we left the room and the company.

CHAPTER 38

COMING OUT

Suzan and I were now in a position to concentrate on Rhode Island Coastal Homes. The only issue was that she wanted me to remain male in our business life. I complied as much as possible, but it was increasingly difficult to do so. It was hard to have female genitalia, be on female hormones for over two years, and have a substantial amount of facial hair removed and pretend that I was still a man. And of course I longed to live 100 percent as a female.

One of the problems we experienced was cash flow. When we sold a property, the income was terrific but most of it went to pay off debts that had built up while we were trying to sell the property. We had a good number of properties on our books and there were some buyers we were helping, but the market was tough. Owners had to be persuaded that their properties were not worth what they thought and when offers came in, they were unwilling to negotiate. One of my thoughts was to start another business to be run alongside RICH, which would be more cash flow friendly. Rhode Island has a large percentage of second homes, mainly on the coast. I had been a part-owner of a second home on the Isle of Wight and in Northern Michigan, so I know how hard it is to find competent people to help with any problem that arises. I decided to help people with their second homes in the area. If they needed a contractor I would find them and oversee the work. If they needed a home cleaned after it had been rented, I could help out there. If they were coming for a visit themselves, I was there to stock their refrigerator with whatever they wanted. If a storm hit the area I could check on their property. Of course, if they wanted to rent out their property, we were perfectly positioned to do that as well. So with these ideas, Second Homes First was born. There was no pretense necessary to run this business, and I was free to be myself. Like most new businesses, the success was not quick to come, but it was growing and I was building a good reputation. Cash was beginning to flow again, this time in a positive direction.

Things between Suzan and I were not that great. We never argued, and we worked well together on our business, but she saw me, her husband, disappearing. It was hard on her, very hard. It wasn't that easy on me either. I had arranged a trip to England again to see my aging mother. I was close to my mother and before she became incapacitated by age, she used to visit us often and I used to go to England at least once a year. On this particular trip I decided it was time to tell my siblings about my situation. For some reason I can't explain, I was in tears each time I told my story. I first saw David, my elder brother, who sat there motionless, rather dumbfounded I think. When I finished telling him he said, "Well if that's what you want, I guess that's okay!"

I felt like saying, "It's not what I want, but it's the way I was born," but didn't. Obviously, it is stunning news, and I need to let the recipient have time to let it sink in. I told him that I now wanted to be known as Sarah, to which he nodded in agreement. Other than obvious minor sibling rivalry, I have always got on very well with all my siblings and this was now proving to be a huge asset.

Next stop was my sister Neenie. She was having a dinner party that evening, somewhat in my honour, and I can't remember why, but I needed to tell her just prior to the guests arriving. We were talking in the kitchen and, as usual, I was crying as I told her. There were people outside arriving so we finished the conversation in her bedroom. "Wow, that's a surprise!" she exclaimed and asked a dozen questions, all of which I answered. After that my mind was blank for the whole evening, which may have had more to do with the generous libations and wonderful food that are always served at Neenie's dinner parties.

Onto Remenham outside Henley-on-Thames where my sister Jayne and her husband Nigel live. They have a truly lovely house there overlooking the river Thames. After dinner we were sitting chatting, and I started my monologue. As usual, I started to tear up. They sat there aghast, then Jayne started to cry along with me. We chatted for a while as I answered their many questions, and when we were finished Nigel got up to get himself another drink and said, "Well, I think you are very brave." I really didn't see it that way at all. To me it was something that just had to be done and damn the consequences.

And then there was my brother John who lives in Perth, Australia. Like the situation with Jeremy, it was not possible to let him know face-to-face, and I didn't think a phone call was the way to go, so I wrote to him. Like everyone else I'm sure he was shocked and bewildered. But like my other siblings he quickly came to accept me for who I am, not what I am.

Around Christmastime I felt it was time to "come out" to my friends. I was now living full time as Sarah, all my family knew, and I saw no reason to hide anything. After all, I had the surgery nine months prior. The reactions were mostly predictable: everyone was shocked, some in awe and some disgusted. The most pleasant surprise came from my old schoolmates David Howell, Pete Laing, and Phil Soskin. We had all been jocks and enjoyed each other's banter, locker room chatter, and jokes. I felt sure that they would be polite and drift away, not wanting to be associated with me anymore. In reality, quite the opposite happened. They were incredible. It almost felt that they circled around me to protect me. They were supportive and caring, even if they didn't understand it.

On the other hand, I had some very close friends, Ed and Sandi. They initially lived next door to us in Troy, Michigan and we had hit it off immediately. They had lived in England for a couple of years, as Ed's company had asked him to work there, so they had an understanding of us as Europeans. We went out to dinner together often, and they invited us to their golf club, which was always delightful. They had no children, so for many years, we invited them into our home, often including her mother, for Christmas dinner and a gift exchange.

Sandi was always rather loud, self-centered and eccentric, and even though several people question why we would be friends, we were. Not only that, they were our best friends. We helped each other in many ways, as friends do. When the children were young, we named them guardians should anything happen to us. So you can imagine my shock and surprise when they completely shunned me. They absolutely refused to talk to me or write to me as I had to them. They didn't want to understand or even try to come to grips with the situation and that state of affairs remains to this day. They pretend to be caring, loving Christian people but that's just a facade and their position is absolutely untenable.

Now I was "out" to friends and family, that was a huge relief. For the first time I was completely free to be myself, to be Sarah. Those who did not try to understand my predicament were now dead to me and I didn't spend an ounce of energy on them. The others were accepting, some even loving and embracing, even though many didn't understand it. I would be lying if I said coming out wasn't stressful but it had to be done and now I have a whole new life ahead of me.

PART 8
A NEW LIFE

CHAPTER 39

THE SPLIT

I t was now mid-winter, cold and miserable in Rhode Island. The talk and chatter between old friends and Suzan had been relentless. Opinions differed widely. I was not party to the conversations nor did I want to be. But in some part I think it led to Suzan asking me for a divorce. This was totally understandable and expected. Even though I tried to argue that it didn't have to happen and that there were several instances where wives of post-op transsexuals stayed with their partners, Suzan was having none of it. She just said that unlike her, those women were too dependent. There was no argument from me, just sorrow in my heart at the inevitable. We calmly talked things through. I told her of a very good, inexpensive attorney who would help her, and we agreed to divide everything equally. As an uncontested divorce, it all went through very quickly and smoothly. When the divorce papers finally arrived, Suzan asked me how I felt. I said that it's just a piece of paper and my feelings remain just as they always have.

But now we were to live our separate lives. Suzan decided to go back to nursing school and become a State Enrolled Nurse (SEN), as she was in England, and keep her real estate business going as much as possible. I felt that she should become a Registered Nurse (RN) because she was capable of passing the exams, but her confidence level was telling her differently. She found herself a small one-bedroom, ground floor apartment with a garden at the side. It was a particularly good find, as it was able to house her large antique dining room furniture, which I let her have prior to the equal splitting of property.

As for me, I needed and wanted to head south to a warmer climate. I searched on the internet all over Florida for a place, preferably on the coast with a low cost of living and a low housing cost. I came across Palm Coast on the east coast, north of Daytona Beach and south of St. Augustine. Everything there looked good, so I decide to drive to Florida and check the place out. Sure enough, it was everything I was looking for. It's a newish town, well laid out, and on the coast with ridiculously low housing costs. The whole of the U.S. was in a housing slump, and Florida and California were the hardest hit. When I returned home, I knew that was where I wanted to live. I found a new, three-bedroom duplex with a two-car garage for rent at only $800 per month. Perfect. So I rented it sight unseen.

I was obsessing somewhat about how I would feel when I finally had to say goodbye to Suzan. I could see myself bawling my eyes out until I reached the Connecticut boarder, about an hour's drive. Over the next few days we were busy separating our belongings and then with the help of Suzan, I finally loaded the truck and strapped my car on the trailer. The time had come. Few words were said; I think we were both mentally and physically drained. I looked back at Suzan with tears in my eyes, unable to talk. I waved goodbye and walked out of the door. There was no bawling, just a tear or two, and then I was concentrated on getting the vehicle to Florida.

It's a two-day drive with an overnight stop in the Richmond, Virginia area. I finally reached my destination in Palm Coast and had a room booked at a local hotel. For dinner, I decided to go to the restaurant next door and had a small meal. Walking back to the hotel, I suddenly had the loneliest feeling I've ever felt. This was now my hometown, and I knew nobody, absolutely nobody, and nobody knew me. Those in other cities who knew me, like my family, had only a rough idea of where I was. It was a desperate feeling, but one of my own making. Once back in my room I checked my emails and there was one from my sister Jayne wishing me a safe journey and all the best in my new home. That was a huge uplift for me, and I immediately wrote back and told her so. From that point on I felt fine: no more self-pity, no more doubts, I was exactly where I wanted and needed to be.

The rental home was perfect in every respect. It was brand new, spacious, and clean as a whistle. I soon settled in and the furniture I had fit perfectly. This was home, and it was lovely. I needed a job and decided against getting my real estate license in Florida. It meant starting all over again from the beginning, and I knew exactly the financial outlay and time it took before there is an income flow.

The Home Depot is a DIY store that I frequently visited. There was a sign outside stating that they were hiring and to inquire inside, so I did. I was thinking that I could help them in hardware or in the garden center, but they were looking for cashiers. Whatever. A job is a job. Even though it was part time, they were giving benefits, including health care. Well, it wasn't exactly being the Vice President of Operations of a multi-national corporation for the Eastern U.S. and Ontario (which of course I never mentioned to them), but it was a job, so I took it. My social security was about to kick in, and so living on my own I was able to make ends meet.

As a side note, transsexuals are always warned that after they go through the change they can expect a drop in income. Nowadays, it's not as bad as it has become more acceptable and it is illegal in the U.S. to let someone go on the basis of gender. However, employers can make life uncomfortable, and if the employee leaves then she will have a difficult time trying to find a position at the same wage or salary level. I actually rather enjoyed being a cashier, and it was good for me to interact with customers as a female and build up my confidence. The Home Depot seemed to like me, as they made me a full-time employee fairly quickly, which was unusual. Mind you, I didn't put up with any corporate nonsense, as I knew that side very well. Whereas other employees would meekly bow to ridiculous requests and rules, I would challenge them if I felt they were unreasonable or ludicrous, no matter whom they were. I think I gained their respect very quickly, although I didn't want to move up in the company. I was happy doing what I was doing: there was little to no stress, I could build up my self-confidence, and made many friends within the company.

Living as a female 100 percent of the time was fun; even exhilarating. Life seemed so much gentler and happier. Just walking down a street was a different experience. Men smiled at you, women smiled at you, too, in different ways of course. This rarely happens in a man's world. I quickly became accustomed to having doors opened for me or being waited on first in a restaurant. The sun had risen on my new life, and it was beautiful. There was a lot to get used to, but they were all good things.

One time I was in a long checkout line at a store. Slowly, I had worked my way close to the front of the line. There was a cashier who came to open another register and then called out, "Ma'am, I can help you over here." Again she said, "Ma'am, I can help you here." There was a tap on my arm and the lady behind me said "you can go over there".

A little startled, I moved to the other register and thought "Oh yes, shit, ma'am, that's me now!"

CHAPTER 40

MORE SURGERY

There were just two more things I needed to address. One of the most expensive and dramatic procedures a transsexual can undertake is Facial Feminization Surgery (FFS). I carried out a great deal of research on FFS, knowing that my rather masculine looking face needed some work. There are only a few surgeons that specialize in this work in the U.S. and they are very expensive. I knew of several in Thailand that carried out the procedure that were somewhat less expensive but, unlike my Sex Reassignment Surgery, I did not know anyone who had undergone this type of surgery in Thailand.

One of the best-known surgeons, if not the best, was Dr. Jeffery Spiegel in Boston. I heard that he was giving a general presentation in Florida so I went along to hear him. After the presentation he was giving fairly quick individual consultations, and he advised me that I would greatly benefit from FFS. On my next visit to see Deb's family and Suzan in New England I made an appointment to have a full consultation with Dr. Spiegel. He went through all the separate procedures he could carry out to make me look more feminine — almost a dozen! He said his assistant would write them up and cost them out for me, and I could decide what I wanted done. All of the procedures totaled $50,000 in 2012. Even though that's just the surgeon's bill, for the amount of work to be done, I didn't think it was too bad. The Thailand option was appealing from a cost point of view, and I knew the hospitals there to be excellent, but did I really want to risk my forever look to a surgeon I knew nothing about in a place where I had no recourse?

When I was back home, I thought hard about the procedures I felt I needed. The better approach for me was to delete the ones I didn't need or want to have done. This included a nose job, as my nose had been broken three times before and the thought of going through that again was too much. The other major procedure I eliminated was changing my jaw line. Generally, women's faces are narrower in the jaw than men and it does certainly look more feminine, but I didn't think it totally necessary and seemed rather drastic. Dr. Sanguan had already shaved my trachea when I had my SRS. The one item I didn't have done but somewhat regret is cheek implants. In retrospect I think it would have helped my looks for the better.

However, what I did have done was still substantial. The bone structure over men's eyes tends to bulge out and can be very pronounced. It's called bossing, and Dr. Spiegel said that even though mine wasn't that pronounced, I would definitely benefit from having the bone shaved there. My eyebrows and my eyelids definitely need work, as did my very thin lip. And with all this work I was given a general face-lift. I sent my list of suggested surgeries to Boston and was accepted as a patient with a surgery date in early May.

I had mentioned the possibility of surgery to both Deb and Suzan. Deb was not happy about it and felt I looked fine the way I was; Suzan really didn't say anything. At the time, it seemed that I couldn't count on them for support, so I booked myself into a Marriott Hotel by the Constitution. It was a studio-type room with a kitchenette and living area, which was perfect as I was to be there for nine days. I also needed someone to check me out of the hospital (not a cab driver!) and take me to my hotel. It was recommended that I have a nurse to change my dressing for the first couple of days, so I arranged for nursing care who also acted as my chauffeur.

Everything was set. The surgery was to be done at a major Boston hospital and I would spend one night there and then be released. After checking into the hotel, I had a final meeting with Dr. Spiegel to go over the procedures in general terms. If he had told me in detail what he was about to do to me, I think I would have been on the first plane back to Florida.

After an early check-in at the hospital, I was prepared for the surgery and met the doctor in his scrubs just prior to going into the operating room. He asked if I had any questions and thinking of Deb I said, "Just carry out the changes in moderation please."

I came around in the recovery area, but the first thing I remember was in my room. A nurse came in and dumped the call button on my bed.

"This is your call button," she said abruptly and walked out of the room.

I was basically blind from the swelling and had a mass of bandages around my head. I fumbled around and eventually found it. About 10 minutes later the phone rang. Again, I fumbled around and stretched out to where the sound was coming from. Surprisingly, I found it and was able to say a feeble hello.

"What do you want for dinner," a rather curt voice said.

That was absolutely the last thing I was thinking about and said "Oh, nothing, thank you."

"Well you have to have something," the voice said.

"Okay, what are my choices?" I mumbled.

"You can have anything you want," she continued. Picking up on my total disinterest, she said "How about some lovely mashed potatoes and gravy," softening her tone somewhat.

To me that sounded disgusting, but I said, "That's fine, thank you very much."

Dinner arrived and a tiny taste told me not to eat any more. I drank the juice and pushed the table away.

What I needed was rest, so I laid back and noticed though the crack in my eyelid that my drip was not dripping! I found my call button and pushed it.

Five minutes passed and no one came so I pushed the call button again. I know that they are busy, but what if this was an emergency? Eventually a male nurse strolls in and says, in a very off hand way, "What's up?" I told him about the drip, and he all but accused me of doing something to it. He fiddled around with it, got it going and strolled out without saying another word.

The after effects of the anesthetic were now beginning to catch up with me. I was feeling nauseous but couldn't find a bowl, so I pushed the call button again, and again I waited and waited. Eventually a nurse comes in and I told her I needed a bowl, as I felt nauseous. "It's right here," she said rather annoyed. "Oh! Where is it," she continued, "it's supposed to be here." She went scurrying around my bed to the locker and said, "Oh, I found it" and gave it to me. I promptly threw up!

It seemed to me that everyone hated their job and had no interest in looking after their patients. Their attitude was appalling as was their care, which was rudimentary at best.

The patient in the next room was on a heart monitor. Strangely I found the rhythmic beat quite soothing, then the rhythm changed and became erratic for a short while and then flat lined! OMG! I again went to my call button feeling that this was a real emergency, as obviously the person next door could not call the nursing staff. As usual, no one came. Eventually someone came and the flat line noise was still going, so I told them the noise was preventing me from sleeping and I asked to speak to the head nurse of the unit. Inside, I was really fuming about the lack of care especially as I was paying thousands of dollars to be there for my elective surgery.

When the head nurse arrived I told her in the strongest terms possible how unhappy I was and gave her all the examples. I said that if things didn't improve immediately that I would check myself out, as the care at my hotel was infinitely better than in the hospital! She was somewhat sympathetic but said it was not possible to check myself out. I promised her I would leave if things didn't improve, and I meant it. I'm sure she spoke to her staff as one of the nurses came in almost in tears and apologized.

The next day the private nurse delivered me to my hotel room. I walked past the reception area looking like a mummy with all my bandages.

"What do you want me to do now?" she asked. I felt like saying you're the f---ing nurse, I'm just a patient. Again, I was paying all this money for a top quality private nurse, and they hadn't a clue what to do. I asked her to come back tomorrow and change my dressing. Conversely, the hotel staff was absolutely fantastic. They called up to my room about twice a day to start with, just to check to see if I was all right and if there was anything I needed or that they could do for me. They gave me little gifts throughout my stay and a card signed by all of them with another gift at the end of my stay. Wonderful, caring people!

The actual procedure that Dr. Spiegel carried out was to cut behind and in front of my ears and around my hairline so that he could pull the whole skin forward to expose the eyebrow bone, which he then shaved down. He cut my eyelids so that he could give them a lift and under my nose and the corners of my mouth so that he could reshape my lips. Then he pulled everything up to rid my face of any excess skin. I lost the feeling in my scalp for about a year but other than that there were no lasting scars or uncomfortable feelings. I was delighted with the outcome, as was Suzan, who thought I looked much better. I really do feel that Dr. Spiegel is the best in the business and am so happy that I did not go to Thailand to have the FFS, although I'm quite sure that the nursing care there would have been exceptional.

The only other surgery I was considering was breast augmentation. The female hormones I was taking gave me some breast tissue and with a padded bra my figure was reasonably good, but like most women, I wanted to have better-looking breasts. I heard from several women that the saline solution implants were not very satisfactory. They neither looked nor felt natural. Fortunately, the silicone implants were back on the market after being banned for a while. It was erroneously thought that leaking implants caused cancer or lupus. I knew that Dr. Sanguan performed many breast augmentations and so wrote to him to get costs. Compared to the other procedures I had, this was really quite minor. Dates and times were set, so I was off to Phuket, Thailand for the second time.

The doctor's chauffeur picked me up again and dropped me off at the hotel next to the International Hospital. I didn't realize at the time, but the construction going on during my previous visit was for a new hospital, the old one having been torn down. His clinic inside the hospital was very chic and full of women seeking breast augmentation for one reason or another. Fortunately, I was one of the first to see him.

I was quite specific about what I wanted. My new breasts were not to be too large, oval in shape, with the incisions to be under the breast. The oval shape is a little more expensive, but so much more realistic. I always think that the round ones look false and are a dead giveaway. So using a special bra I tried several sizes and chose one. Dr. Sanguan was surprised by my choice, as I think he normally sees women who want the biggest available. I know many women really regretted going for extra-large breasts.

So the procedure was done and as the doctor wanted to see me again in a week, I stayed in the center of Phuket enjoying my new look. He was pleased with his work, as was I. Soon I was on my way again.

One of my old school buddies, David Howell, lives with his Thai wife, Ing, in Bangkok and Hua Hin on the east coast. When I had my first surgery, I didn't think it appropriate to contact him to let him know. We hadn't seen each other since our very early 20s, and I didn't know how he would react. Since then, I had let him know of my change, and he was naturally shocked but very understanding. So after this latest surgery, I arranged to stay with him and Ing in Hua Hin. The reunion after 45 years was amazing. We picked up where we left off and had the most wonderful time together.

CHAPTER 41

LIVING A NIGHTMARE

Life was good, I enjoyed Palm Coast, especially the Flagler Beach area. The larger cities to the north and south had much to offer: St. Augustine, the oldest city in the U.S., had many good restaurants and many historic sites to visit; and Daytona Beach had the Speedway race track and many shops that were fun to visit. One day, I received a call from Jeremy. He and his new girlfriend Megan — he and wife had divorced — were going to visit her dad in Flagler Beach where he had a second home, and they would like to come and visit.

"Of course," I said, "that would be wonderful" and so we set up a date. They were scheduled to come after lunch, spend the night and leave the next morning.

The thought of having my first visitors, especially family, was awesome. I was excited to meet Megan for the first time, so I went out and purchased a load of food to make a great meal. They arrived mid-afternoon, and I had purposely dressed down for Jeremy. After the initial introduction and a superficial hug that Jeremy gave me, he looked at my beige Capri pants and tugged on them saying, "what's this" in a disgusted tone. This isn't a good start, I thought but made light of it. I showed them around the house and then we sat and chatted for a short while. I then suggested we go for a walk around the neighborhood, which Megan readily agreed to, although Jeremy was a little reluctant. During the walk Jeremy said he was looking forward to having Chinese food tonight. I had built up a reputation in my family for cooking excellent Chinese food.

"Oh!" I said, "I had planned on something else, but if you want to have Chinese, I'm sure I have enough ingredients to do a Chinese dinner." Anything to keep the peace, I thought.

"That's good," he replied. "We'll have Chinese."

When we arrived back at the house, I offered them both a drink — they each had a beer. I told them to help themselves to anything they wanted and showed them where everything was kept.

"I better get started with the dinner," I said enthusiastically, "There is a lot of prep work in Chinese cooking, but the good thing is that it only takes a short time to cook."

I started peeling, chopping, slicing and dicing, chatting to them while I was doing it.

"Dad," said Jeremy. "I felt really uncomfortable on our walk just now."

"Why were —" I couldn't finish what I wanted to say.

"You know everybody was staring at us, at you, don't you?"

"No, they weren't, Jeremy. That's just your imagin—"

"Yes, they were, Dad, you just don't see it, do you? You don't see it!" he reiterated, raising his voice.

"No, I don't Jeremy, I have several friends in the neighborhood, and they don't feel uncomfortable in my presence. I meet hundreds people every day at Home Depot, and they don't feel uncomfortable, I'm sure of that."

I was really annoyed that Jeremy had chosen to take this approach with me, especially in front of Megan, or maybe it was because of Megan's presence that he was taking this approach. I just don't know. What I did know was that it was very unpleasant, but I wanted to do everything possible to diffuse the situation. I could see that he was angry, very angry, and I suppose in many respects he had good reason to be. I felt strongly that I should just keep my cool and let him vent and get it out of his system.

As the evening progressed, it got worse. The more he drank the louder and more belligerent he became. He was shouting and crying at times and smoking heavily, which I had never seen him do before. As much as I tried to answer his nonsensical questions, he was not in a listening mood. He was rude and crude. I knew he was really hurt inside, but this was three years after I had first told him. He was 35 years old and should have been able to cope better than this. The alcohol had definitely loosened his tongue, and I really felt it was best to let him roll. The only time he really hurt me verbally was when he said I was just a very selfish individual with no thought for anyone else. To the contrary, I feel that I put everyone else first before taking care of myself. I let his comment go by without saying anything. I felt so sorry for Megan who had to sit through this tirade all evening. We had finished the meal and I had cleaned up, but he was still going.

"I've had enough of this. I'm going to bed, goodnight," I quietly said and went to my bedroom.

Needless to say, I had a restless night and dreaded the morning. But when it came, I just made coffee and waited for them to appear, determined to be social and, as much as possible, understanding. The effects of the alcohol had worn off and everyone was polite, but it was still somewhat tense. They had a bite to eat, packed their bags, and were ready to go. Megan said a heartfelt thank you, gave me a hug, and headed to the car to give Jeremy and me a moment alone. To be totally honest, I can't remember what was said between us, but it was cordial. No apologies from either of us, no harsh words, just a gentle goodbye and it was over. I watched them drive away wondering if I would ever see them again.

My daughter Deb's approach to me couldn't have been more different than Jeremy's. Of course she would have preferred if I hadn't made the change, but after my operation, she got with the program and embraced me as Sarah. The question arose as to how I should be known within their family. Their daughter Julia, my granddaughter, was only 1 year old when I made the decision to make the change, but she saw me as her grandpa until four years old. Obviously out in public it was inappropriate and embarrassing for me to be called Dad and Grandpa, so it was decided that everyone would call me Sarah, which was fine by me — it is my name after all.

CHAPTER 42

ALL'S WELL...

Passion (n.) A strong and barely controllable emotion.

I have a passion for sailing. It's been my passion all my life, but with children and a non-sailing wife, it was a suppressed feeling. Each year, when my family asked for my birthday or Christmas list, I would always put at the top of my list "a 36-foot sailing boat"! But it never arrived.

But now, living on my own, I decided it was time to treat myself to a sailing boat. I purchased a 35-foot O'Day named "Liberty" and sailed her solo on several long trips. One such trip took me across Florida on several waterways and Lake Okeechobee to Ft Myers then onto Key West and back up the south and east side of the Keys.

After a somewhat debauched lifestyle in Marathon, it was onto Key Largo to meet up with Jeremy and Megan, who were coming in from Colorado. The weather for the next week was expected to be good, which was a change from what I had been experiencing. It had been a record breaking low of 48°F and windy the day before; not very pleasant.

Jeremy and Megan planned on staying a couple of days with me on the boat before heading back home. His feelings toward me had greatly improved. While in the pool he confided in me that he had started a new website to help the consumers of marijuana. The state of Colorado had recently legalized marijuana and his site was to guide users as to where to buy, where to stay and what to do, such as tours of the growers and to understand the laws. Much to his surprise, I was very supportive, seeing no harm in advising users. He purposely hadn't told Suzan or me for fear of retribution. I told him not to worry and that I would let Suzan know and was sure that she would be okay with it too.

Currently, the site is doing very well since several other states have followed Colorado's and Washington State's lead. Jeremy and Megan's visit was very pleasant, and we had a good time together sightseeing, eating out, and enjoying a beer or two. I was sorry to see them leave.

Docked next to Liberty was a 28-foot powerboat. The owner was staying on it for a while and was very helpful when I first arrived. He told me all the ins and outs of the marina as each has their own set of rules, gate codes, and amenities. Most nights, we chatted across the dock separating us and it turns out that he was a good looking Hungarian named Roland who spoke perfect English.

The last night I was there I was having a steak off my grill that was much too large for me to eat, so I invited Roland over. At first he refused but then with a little encouragement he accepted the offer. He was always complimentary about the way I looked and dressed, very flattering. After the meal — which I have to say was delicious — he came over to sit beside me in the cockpit. We chatted some more when he suggested we go down inside the boat. There we finished off the evening in the most delightful way with the help from KY jelly!

After 77 days and 896 miles, Liberty and I finally arrived at Palm Coast Marina. I was tired but happy, having learned a great deal about myself and made several improvements to Liberty along the way. I met the most wonderful people, saw extraordinary sights, crossed the tricky Lake Okeechobee, experienced the beautiful Gulf Coast and the length of the incomparable Keys, and scared myself to death more times than I care to remember.

Every day was a learning experience, which I'm sure is the same for a novice solo sailor like me or an experienced blue water sailor. However, when all is said and done, the highlight was meeting up with my son Jeremy in Key Largo. Time is a great healer and all wounds that had been created in my family from my change have now healed, although Jeremy still has some scars. Suzan and I continue to be the best of friends and speak to each other at least twice a week, and I stay with her when I am visiting the New England area. We have both adjusted well to living alone and very much doubt that either of us will have another partner.

There is nothing quite like a loving family.

FINAL THOUGHTS

Some people may think how wonderful it is to have lived as both a male and then a female. I can assure you, it is not. Interesting maybe, but frankly, I would much prefer to have been born 100 percent male or 100 percent female, rather than stuck in the middle. The truth is that you are never one or the other, however many psychiatrists or operations you have. You are transsexual. End of story.

Having said that, I have to say that I am very happy living my life as a female. I feel comfortable with my body and way of life. I realize I am not the most feminine female. On the contrary, some would say I'm rather butch, but that's the way I'm built! I am content.

Transsexuals (TS) are very slowly becoming more accepted into society. Of the LGBT alumni we are the least accepted. There are no known finite numbers for the amount of TS people in the U.S., Europe, or anywhere for that matter, which is somewhat understandable considering how hard it is to truly diagnose TS as opposed to transgender. However, I would have thought it possible to easily count the number of TS patients who have had Sex Reassignment Surgery. In the U.K. however, it is estimated that there are 2,000 transsexuals.[7] That equates to approximately one in 30,000 or

---

7. David Batty, The Guardian, August 2004

0.003 percent. Whatever the number, it's a very small fraction of a percentage of the population.

That is why this whole bathroom issue in schools is so ridiculous and why a United States president needs to be involved is beyond me. The number of TS pupils in schools is miniscule. They do not go to their chosen sex bathroom or locker rooms to look at other pupils or cause problems. On the contrary, they want to meld in and be as inconspicuous as possible. TS individuals have been around as long as mankind has been around and have never willingly caused a bathroom problem. It's just incredible that suddenly the media is jumping all over a non-issue and legislative bodies around the country start passing legislation.

What is not helpful to our cause are the flamboyant extroverts that exaggerate everything physically whether in parades, carnivals, or just want publicity. The media always publishes photos of those individuals when discussing TS. To me it would be like talking about the glass ceiling for women and in the article showing pictures of girls dancing on poles. There is no connection. It is not what any TS person I have ever met is like or wants to be. We just want to meld into society the best we can.

Bipolar depression is a serious problem and needs to be addressed by a psychiatrist who can administer the appropriate drugs. It is not possible for a bipolar patient to overcome their depression without the proper medication. In my particular case, and every case is different, I only need a small daily dose. However, without it I soon find myself sliding downhill. As you have read, my lows go to the extreme but my high periods do not necessarily go that high. I do not get overly exuberant. When I'm in an up period, I tend to think really positively, which for the most part is very beneficial.

In contrast to transsexualism, bipolar disorder affects 5.7 million people in the U.S., or about 2.6 percent of the population over 18 years old.[8] It is a

---

8. National Institute of Mental Health

serious and debilitating disease. Unfortunately, the stigma that the disease carries prevents a large number of sufferers from getting the treatment they need. What really infuriates me is when a heinous crime is committed, and in the aftermath someone will try to justify it by saying "Well, of course that person suffers from bipolar depression," as if all bipolar sufferers are criminals. Not only is it unlikely that the person was bipolar, but it puts a stigma on bipolar suffers. It is possible that severe bipolar suffers can become violent but to constantly use it as an excuse is indefensible. Bipolar suffers have enough to deal with without having a possible criminal label attached to them.

Both the transsexualism and the bipolar depression that I suffer from are issues that I was born with. Neither of them are identifiable at birth but become apparent at a later date. In my case, the transsexualism around five years old and the bipolar in my late teens. No one questions that a person is born with whatever it is that makes one a bipolar victim, so why does everyone question the validity of being born a transsexual? So many "professionals" state that it is a learned condition. Total bunk, poppycock!

So how do I feel about my life? Generally, I have been very fortunate to be surrounded by the most wonderful people, not only within my family but also my friends, colleagues, and some professionals. Sure, it hasn't been easy. At times it's even been extremely difficult. Whenever I found myself up against a wall or facing impossible odds, I always brought to mind the motto on the Bamford Coat of Arms: Perseverantia Vincit, Perseverance Conquers. It has helped me enormously. But whatever problems I have faced, the only way I know how to deal with them is head on. It helps immensely to have a good sense of humor. As Henry Ward Beecher said, "A person without a sense of humor is like a wagon without springs. It's jolted by every pebble on the road." Mind you at the depth of depression it is impossible to find any humor. The only way out for me is to convince myself that things will improve in time.

Overall, I have had a very good life. I have enjoyed my family, especially watching the children grow into responsible, hardworking individuals. My career in commercial property management and development was especially rewarding, not only in monetary terms but also in terms of subjective well-being. It has been an amazing journey. Going through a sex change has its awkward moments, but knowing that it is absolutely the appropriate thing to do and the only way to be truly fulfilled meant that it was ultimately the right decision for me.

ABOUT THE AUTHOR

Sarah Hartley is retired and lives in Palm Coast, FL. She still follows her passion and keeps her sailing boat *Windsong* in Massachusetts, close to her daughter, Deb, and best friend, Suzan, both of whom also enjoy the boating scene. Sarah loves to travel and has made numerous trips, mainly overseas. Her other loves include writing — currently a book on her genealogy — and gardening, where she prefers to enjoy the fruits of her labor rather than the labor itself!

To contact Sarah:

email	mssarahhartley@aim.com
Twitter	@mssarahhartley
Facebook	mssarahhartley.13